HOMO SAPIENS: THE DOMINANT SPECIES

By Rayan Darcy

Origins: The Evolution of Homo Species Series

Book 6\6

Copyright © 2024 by Rayan Darcy

All rights reserved. No part of this publication may be reproduced, distributed, or transmitted in any form or by any means, including photocopying, recording, or other electronic or mechanical methods, without the prior written permission of the publisher, except in the case of brief quotations embodied in critical reviews and certain other noncommercial uses permitted by copyright law.

Table of Contents

Introduction

Welcome to "Homo sapiens: The Dominant Species," the sixth and final book in our series exploring the fascinating journey of human evolution. If you haven't read the first five books —"Homo habilis: The Handy Man," "Homo erectus: The First Travelers," "Homo heidelbergensis: The Bridge to Modern Humans," "Denisovans: The Ghosts of the Ancient World," and "Neanderthals: Our Closest Relatives"—we highly recommend starting with them to gain a foundational understanding of the early members of the Genus Homo. Each of these books provides essential context for understanding the evolutionary advancements and adaptations that have shaped our species. However, if you are only interested in the story of Homo sapiens, this book will be sufficient to provide a comprehensive understanding of our journey from prehistoric times to the present day.

In this book, we will delve into the extraordinary journey of Homo sapiens, the species that transformed the world through unparalleled ingenuity and resilience. We will explore our beginnings in Africa, examining the early tools and art we created as hunter-gatherers. From there, we will trace our emergence out of Africa, following the paths our ancestors took as they spread across the globe. We will investigate the revolutionary development of agriculture, which allowed humans to settle and build the first civilizations. Finishing with the start of writing and the dawn of known history, highlighting how these innovations facilitated the recording and transmission of knowledge, enabling the complex societies we recognize today. All this and more will be drawn from the latest scientific research, offering a compelling narrative that is both informative and engaging.

Book Organization

Chapter 1: Homo sapiens Emerge:
This chapter delves into the origins and early development of Homo sapiens. We explore the emergence of our species in Africa, examining the key fossil discoveries and genetic analyses that provide insight into the early days of modern humans. By tracing the timeline and significant sites where Homo sapiens remains have been found, we lay the groundwork for understanding the beginning of our evolutionary journey.

Chapter 2: Prehistoric Tools
 In this chapter, we explore the evolution of tools used by early Homo sapiens. We will examine the various periods and types of tools, from simple stone implements to more advanced creations made from bone, antler, and wood. Additionally, we will delve into the use of fire, the construction of shelters, and the development of early boats. By investigating key archaeological sites and findings, we gain insight into how these technological advancements enhanced survival and shaped human progress.

Chapter 3: Early Art
 This chapter delves into the creative expressions of early Homo sapiens. We will explore cave paintings, carvings, and other forms of early art, examining their significance and what they reveal about the cognitive and cultural development of our ancestors. By studying key archaeological sites and findings, we gain insight into the symbolic and social aspects of early human life.

Chapter 4: Our Emergence Out of Africa:
 This chapter explores the migration of Homo sapiens out of Africa to every continent. We will examine when, how, and why early humans spread to Asia, Europe, Australia, and the Americas.

Chapter 5: The Pro Hunters Period:
 This chapter delves into the Pro Hunters Period, around 15,000 years ago, just before the advent of agriculture. We will explore the advanced hunting tools, techniques, and strategies used by Homo sapiens to hunt various game.

Chapter 6: Story: Bound by Hoofbeats
 This chapter presents a novel-documentary style narrative that aims to help readers understand the experiences and challenges faced by our ancestors while being engaging and enjoyable.

Chapter 7: The Beginnings of Animal Domestication:
 This chapter explores the early stages of animal domestication by Homo sapiens. We will examine when, where, and why different animals were first domesticated, including dogs, sheep, goats, cats and cattle.

Chapter 8: The Start of Agriculture
 This chapter examines the revolutionary transition from hunting and gathering to agriculture. We will explore when and where agriculture first developed, including key regions like the Fertile Crescent, China, and Mesoamerica, and we will see how it changed human societies forever.

Chapter 9: Social Structures and Governance

 This chapter examines the emergence of social structures and governance in early human societies. We will explore how agricultural communities developed complex social hierarchies and systems of governance to manage resources, maintain order, and coordinate communal activities.

Chapter 10: The Great Bottleneck:

 This chapter explores the dramatic near-extinction event known as the Great Bottleneck. Around 70,000 years ago, the human population dwindled to a critical low. We will delve into what caused this event and how our ancestors survived it. You'll be surprised to learn just how close we were to extinction and the incredible resilience that ensured our survival. This event profoundly shaped the genetic diversity of our species and set the stage for the future of human evolution.

Chapter 11: The Dawn of Writing and Recorded History

 This chapter will explore how writing began, the first places it appeared, and its profound effects on human societies. We will discuss the origins of writing in regions such as Mesopotamia and Egypt, and how it revolutionized communication, administration, and culture. The book will conclude at the dawn of known history, marking the end of our journey through prehistory.

 Each chapter in this book aims to provide a comprehensive understanding of Homo sapiens. By the end of this journey, you will have a deeper appreciation of our history.
To start, we need to go back to the very beginning of Homo sapiens' emergence, around 300,000 years ago.

CHAPTER I:

HOMO SAPIENS EMERGE

The Emergence of Homo sapiens:

Around 300,000 years ago, in the heart of Africa, a remarkable transformation was taking place. This was a period of significant climatic shifts, with alternating wet and dry periods shaping the landscape. Vast savannas, interspersed with dense forests and expansive lakes, provided a diverse and resource-rich environment. It was in this dynamic and challenging setting that Homo sapiens, our species, first emerged. These early humans exhibited a combination of physical and behavioral traits that distinguished them from other hominin species. The emergence of Homo sapiens marked a pivotal point in evolutionary history. Unlike their predecessors, early Homo sapiens displayed a unique set of adaptations that allowed them to thrive in varied environments. Their larger brains and more complex social structures gave them a distinct advantage, enabling them to develop advanced tools and strategies for survival. The climatic fluctuations of the time played a crucial role in shaping these adaptations, as early humans were forced to navigate changing landscapes and resource availability. This period of environmental unpredictability likely drove innovation and flexibility, key traits that would become hallmarks of Homo sapiens. These traits not only distinguished them from other hominins but also set the foundation for their future dominance.

Discoveries at Jebel Irhoud:

The Jebel Irhoud site in Morocco is one of the most significant archaeological discoveries related to early Homo sapiens. The fossils found here, dating back approximately 300,000 years, provide a fascinating glimpse into the early development of our species. The remains include a variety of skeletal fragments, with the most notable being a well-preserved skull that exhibits a mix of primitive and modern features. This skull has a large brow ridge, characteristic of earlier hominins, but also a globular braincase, which is a hallmark of modern humans. The blend of these features highlights the transitional nature of early Homo sapiens, bridging the gap between older hominins and contemporary humans. The Jebel Irhoud fossils are not just significant for their age but also for what they tell us about the lifestyle and capabilities of early Homo sapiens. The accompanying stone tools found at the site are part of the Middle Stone Age technology and are more advanced than those of their predecessors. These tools included pointed flakes and blades, indicating a leap in cognitive abilities and manual dexterity. The presence of these tools alongside the fossils implies that early Homo sapiens were capable of complex thought processes and had developed advanced techniques for hunting and processing food. This suggests a level of sophistication in their daily lives and an ability to adapt to their environment in innovative ways.

The Jebel Irhoud findings challenge the previously held notion that Homo sapiens evolved solely in East Africa. Instead, these discoveries suggest a more widespread emergence of our species across the African continent. This has led to a reevaluation of how we understand the origins of Homo sapiens, indicating a pan-African origin rather than a single localized event. The diversity of sites and the spread of early Homo sapiens fossils across Africa underline the importance of regional adaptations and interactions in shaping our species. Each new discovery adds a piece to the puzzle, helping us understand the varied environments in which early Homo sapiens lived and thrived.

Additional Fossil Discoveries:

In addition to the Jebel Irhoud fossils, other significant discoveries have contributed to our understanding of early Homo sapiens. The Omo Kibish fossils from Ethiopia, dated to around 195,000 years ago, are among the earliest evidence of anatomically modern humans. These remains include a partial skull and other skeletal fragments that closely resemble modern human anatomy. The Omo Kibish fossils underscore the idea that Homo sapiens had spread across diverse regions of Africa, adapting to various ecological niches. Similarly, the Herto fossils, also from Ethiopia and dating back about 160,000 years, offer further insights into the anatomical development of Homo sapiens. These fossils include skulls that show a blend of archaic and modern features, much like the Jebel Irhoud remains. The Herto individuals had larger braincases and more pronounced facial features, indicative of continued evolutionary changes within Homo sapiens.

These fossil discoveries are complemented by genetic studies that trace the lineage of modern humans. Advances in DNA analysis have allowed scientists to compare the genomes of contemporary populations with those of ancient humans. These studies suggest that all modern humans share a common ancestry that can be traced back to Africa, supporting the theory of a single origin for Homo sapiens. Genetic evidence also reveals the migration patterns of early humans as they spread out of Africa and into other parts of the world, interacting with and sometimes interbreeding with other hominin species like Neanderthals and Denisovans.

 The emergence of Homo sapiens also brought about significant changes in social behavior and cultural practices. Evidence from archaeological sites suggests that early Homo sapiens lived in small, cohesive groups, relying on cooperation and social bonds for survival. These groups were likely organized around kinship and shared resources, with complex social structures that facilitated communication and cooperation. The cognitive advancements of early Homo sapiens are further evidenced by the emergence of symbolic behavior. This is exemplified by the discovery of engraved ochre pieces and perforated shells at sites like Blombos Cave in South Africa, dating to around 75,000 years ago. These artifacts indicate that early humans engaged in symbolic thought, possibly using these items for personal adornment or ritualistic purposes. Such behaviors reflect the early roots of cultural expression and abstract thinking, traits that would become hallmarks of human societies.

 Homo sapiens' ability to adapt to changing environments was crucial for their survival and eventual dominance. As climate conditions fluctuated, early humans developed strategies to exploit a wide range of resources. They hunted large game, gathered diverse plant foods, and possibly even engaged in fishing and other aquatic activities. This adaptability not only ensured their survival but also facilitated their spread to new regions. The journey of Homo sapiens from their origins in Africa to their eventual spread across the globe is a testament to their resilience and ingenuity. These early humans laid the foundations for the complex societies that would follow, marking the beginning of a remarkable evolutionary journey. The fossils and artifacts left behind provide a window into their world, revealing a species capable of remarkable innovation, social complexity, and cultural expression.

 As we continue to uncover and study these ancient remains, our understanding of Homo sapiens' emergence and early development becomes increasingly detailed. Each new discovery adds to the rich tapestry of our shared human heritage, highlighting the unique combination of traits that set Homo sapiens on the path to becoming the dominant species on Earth. The ongoing research not only sheds light on our past but also informs our understanding of human diversity and adaptation. By piecing together the story of our origins, scientists can better appreciate the evolutionary processes that have shaped who we are today. This knowledge underscores the interconnectedness of all humans and the shared journey that began in the heart of Africa hundreds of thousands of years ago.

CHAPTER 2:
PREHISTORIC TOOLS

300,000-200,000 Years Ago: Early Beginnings:

Around 300,000 years ago, Homo sapiens first emerged in Africa, marking the dawn of a new era in human evolution. This period saw the development of early tools and techniques that would lay the foundation for future advancements. The tools from this era were part of the Middle Stone Age technology and included pointed flakes and blades. These tools were crafted using sophisticated techniques, such as the Levallois method, which involved preparing a core to produce uniformly shaped flakes. This represented a significant leap in cognitive abilities and manual dexterity compared to earlier hominins. The cognitive shift allowed Homo sapiens to engage in more complex tasks and develop a deeper understanding of their environment.

Fire was an essential element in the lives of early Homo sapiens, providing warmth, protection, and a means to cook food. The controlled use of fire dates back much earlier for other hominins, but for Homo sapiens, it was during this period that fire became a crucial part of daily life. Evidence from archaeological sites suggests that early Homo sapiens utilized fire, which played a vital role in their survival. Fire allowed them to cook meat, making it easier to digest and providing more nutrients, which in turn supported brain development. The ability to manage fire enabled Homo sapiens to inhabit colder climates later and protect themselves from predators, giving them a distinct survival advantage. They used fire not only for cooking but also for hardening wooden tools, providing a more versatile and durable set of implements. However, fossil evidence indicating that Homo sapiens had mastered the ability to create fire themselves during this period has not been found.

Shelters during this period were likely temporary structures made from natural materials like wood, leaves, and animal hides. These early shelters provided protection from the elements and predators. Archaeological evidence indicates that Homo sapiens began to establish more permanent settlements near water sources, which offered abundant resources and strategic advantages. These early shelters, while simple, marked the beginning of more complex living arrangements that would evolve over time. The development of these shelters suggests an increasing understanding of construction techniques and a need for stable living environments, reflecting the gradual shift from nomadic lifestyles to more sedentary communities. The presence of tools in these early settlements also suggests that early humans were starting to create designated spaces for specific activities, such as tool-making and food preparation, indicating a more organized and structured way of life.

During the period between 300,000 and 200,000 years ago, Homo sapiens began experimenting with new materials and methods. The use of bone and antler as raw materials for tools became more common. These materials were used to create various implements, such as awls for making holes in hides and bone points for hunting and processing animals. The introduction of these new materials represented a significant step in the diversification of tool-making practices.

However, evidence for the use of composite tools, such as stone points attached to wooden shafts using animal sinew or plant fibers, primarily appears later in the archaeological record. The period between 300,000 and 200,000 years ago was more about the initial diversification and sophistication of tools made from readily available materials like stone, bone, and antler. The innovations in tool-making during this period greatly enhanced the functionality and efficiency of tools, allowing early humans to perform a wider range of tasks more effectively, such as hunting larger game and processing resources more efficiently.

200,000-100,000 Years Ago: Advancements in Tools and Techniques:

Between 200,000 and 100,000 years ago, Homo sapiens experienced a significant era of innovation and adaptation, marked by remarkable advancements in tools and techniques. This period saw the evolution and refinement of Middle Stone Age technology, which included more sophisticated tools such as scrapers, points, and blades. These tools were crafted with a higher degree of precision and skill, indicating a deeper understanding of material properties and more sophisticated methods of production. The improved craftsmanship allowed early humans to perform a wider range of tasks more effectively, from hunting and butchering to processing hides and plant materials.

One of the most critical developments during this period was the advent of controlled fire-starting techniques. While the controlled use of fire dates back much earlier, it was during this era that Homo sapiens are believed to have developed reliable methods for creating fire. This ability to start and maintain fire revolutionized daily life, providing warmth, protection from predators, and a means to cook food. Cooking meat made it easier to digest and more nutritious, which in turn supported brain development. Fire also played a central role in social gatherings, fostering communication and strengthening social bonds within communities

Hunting techniques became more advanced, reflecting an increased understanding of animal behavior and the environment. Homo sapiens developed specialized tools and strategies to hunt larger game, which provided a reliable source of protein and other nutrients. Spears with stone points were used for close-range hunting, while throwing spears and atlatls (spear-throwers) allowed hunters to strike from a distance with greater accuracy and force. These advancements in hunting tools and techniques improved efficiency and success rates, supporting larger and more stable populations. The development of these tools also enabled Homo sapiens to hunt a wider range of prey, thereby increasing the diversity of their diet.

shelters during this period evolved to become more complex and durable, providing better protection from the elements and predators. Early humans began to construct shelters using a combination of natural materials and simple construction techniques. Some evidence suggests that they may have used animal hides to insulate their shelters, offering additional warmth in someplaces and protection. The establishment of more permanent settlements allowed for the development of community structures and the division of labor, laying the groundwork for future societal advancements. These shelters not only provided physical protection but also became centers of social and cultural life, where early humans could gather, collaborate, and share knowledge.

The period between 200,000 and 100,000 years ago also saw significant developments in symbolic behavior and cultural practices. Evidence from archaeological sites indicates that Homo sapiens engaged in activities that required abstract thought and expression. The use of ochre for body decoration and the creation of simple carvings suggests that early humans were capable of symbolic thinking. This period also saw the emergence of more elaborate burial practices, indicating a growing awareness of life, death, and possibly beliefs in an afterlife. These cultural developments reflect an increasing complexity in social interactions and a deepening sense of identity and community among early Homo sapiens.

Overall, the period between 200,000 and 100,000 years ago was characterized by significant technological, social, and cultural advancements. These innovations enabled early humans to adapt to a wide range of environments, establish complex social structures, and develop rich cultural traditions. The combination of these factors contributed to the emergence of Homo sapiens as a dominant species, setting the stage for their further evolution and expansion across the globe.

100,000-50,000 Years Ago: The Dawn of Innovation:

The period between 100,000 and 50,000 years ago marked a transformative phase in the history of Homo sapiens, characterized by significant technological advancements and geographic expansion. This era saw the development of new tools and technologies that greatly enhanced their ability to adapt and thrive in diverse environments.

During this period, Homo sapiens began to explore and settle new territories, moving out of Africa and into the Middle East, Asia, and eventually Europe. This migration was facilitated by their advanced tools and adaptability to different environments. As they encountered new challenges and opportunities, they developed new techniques and technologies to survive and flourish. The spread of Homo sapiens across different continents led to greater diversity in cultural practices and technological innovations. Their movement into new regions was driven by a combination of environmental pressures, population growth, and the search for new resources. This expansion not only allowed them to adapt to various climates and ecosystems but also fostered the exchange of ideas and technologies between different groups.

One of the critical innovations during this time was the construction of simple boats, which allowed early humans to traverse water bodies and explore new lands. Evidence suggests that by around 60,000 years ago, Homo sapiens had reached Australia, indicating their capability to build and use watercraft. This ability to navigate across water not only expanded their geographical range but also opened up new resources and trading opportunities. The construction of boats required advanced planning, knowledge of buoyancy, and the ability to work with materials like wood and reeds. These early watercraft likely consisted of simple rafts or dugout canoes, enabling humans to cross rivers and coastal waters.

Hunting techniques continued to evolve, with the development of more sophisticated weapons such as bows and arrows. Evidence suggests that the use of bow and arrow technology began around 71,000 years ago in Africa. This allowed for more effective hunting strategies and greater success in capturing prey. The invention of the bow and arrow marked a significant leap in hunting technology, providing greater range, accuracy, and lethality. This period also saw the refinement of spear-throwers (atlatls), which allowed hunters to hurl spears with increased speed and precision. These advancements in hunting tools made it possible to target a wider range of animals, including fast-moving and dangerous prey, thereby diversifying the diet and increasing the nutritional intake of early Homo sapiens.

Fishing also became more prominent during this period, as evidenced by the discovery of fishhooks and remains of early boats. These advancements enabled Homo sapiens to exploit a wider range of resources, contributing to their survival and expansion. The ability to fish and utilize aquatic resources added a new dimension to their subsistence strategies, allowing them to inhabit coastal and riverine environments more effectively. This period likely saw the development of techniques for fishing in both freshwater and marine settings, including the use of nets, weirs, and traps.

Fire remained a central element of daily life, but its use became more specialized. Early humans developed techniques for controlling and managing fire, using it not only for cooking and warmth but also for modifying their environment. Controlled burns were likely used to clear land, drive game, and promote the growth of certain plants. The ability to manipulate fire in these ways demonstrated a deepening understanding of their environment and the development of complex ecological knowledge. Fire was also essential in the creation of more durable tools, as it was used to harden wooden implements and in the processing of other materials.

Shelters during this period became more sophisticated and varied. Early in this period, Homo sapiens built basic buildings, with the first of these found in Mesopotamia in West Asia. These early shelters expanded to become small towns with organized communities. By the end of this period, walled settlements had developed, with protective walls playing a crucial role in towns like Jericho in Palestine, which kept approximately 3,000 inhabitants safe. Early cities also began to emerge in Rome, marking the transition from simple settlements to complex urban centers. Evidence suggests that Homo sapiens built structures from a combination of materials, including wood, stone, and animal hides. These shelters provided better protection from the elements and predators, supporting more stable and permanent settlements. The development of semi-permanent and permanent dwellings allowed for greater social organization and the accumulation of resources, laying the foundation for future agricultural societies. The construction of these shelters required cooperation and coordination, reflecting an increasingly complex social structure.

The cognitive and cultural advancements of Homo sapiens during this period are also evident in the development of art and symbolic behavior. The creation of cave paintings, carvings, and other forms of artistic expression suggests a rich and complex cultural life. These artworks often depicted animals, hunting scenes, and abstract symbols, reflecting both the daily life and the spiritual beliefs of early humans. The use of symbolic artifacts, such as beads and pendants, indicates the importance of social identity and status within early human communities. This period also saw the emergence of ritualistic behaviors and early forms of religion, as evidenced by the burial of the dead with grave goods and the creation of sacred spaces.

Metalworking also began to make its appearance during this period, though it was in its very early stages. The ability to work with metal marked a significant technological advancement, as it allowed for the creation of more durable and effective tools and ornaments. Early metalworking involved the use of native metals like copper and gold, which could be hammered into shape without smelting. This skill laid the groundwork for future metallurgical developments that would become more prominent in later periods. The oldest known gold treasure was found in Bulgaria, hidden underground for 6,000 years, showcasing the early use of metals for ornamental purposes.

The very first writing systems also began to emerge toward the end of this period, marking the transition from prehistory to recorded history. Both Egyptian hieroglyphs and Sumerian cuneiform in Mesopotamia represent some of the earliest forms of writing. This development allowed for the recording of transactions, events, and stories, marking the beginning of known history and the end of the prehistoric era.

Overall, the period from 100,000 to 50,000 years ago was marked by significant technological, social, and cultural advancements that set the stage for the continued expansion and success of Homo sapiens. These innovations enabled early humans to adapt to a wide range of environments, establish complex social structures, and develop rich cultural traditions. The combination of these factors contributed to the emergence of Homo sapiens as the dominant species on Earth. This era laid the groundwork for the agricultural revolution and the rise of complex civilizations that would follow in the millennia to come.

CHAPTER 3:
EARLY ART

The cognitive and cultural advancements of Homo sapiens from their earliest expressions of art to the construction of the first pyramids are remarkable milestones in human history. This chapter will explore the evolution of art and symbolic behavior from its inception to the creation of monumental architecture, reflecting the profound developments in human creativity, spirituality, and social complexity.

The Dawn of Artistic Expression:

The earliest known art created by Homo sapiens dates back to around 100,000 years ago. Evidence from archaeological sites such as Blombos Cave in South Africa reveals that early humans engaged in complex symbolic activities. Engraved pieces of ochre with geometric patterns and shell beads used for personal ornamentation are among the earliest examples of abstract thought and artistic expression. These artifacts suggest that early humans used symbols to convey social status, identity, and possibly even to communicate ideas. The beads were carefully crafted, with small holes drilled into them for stringing, demonstrating advanced skills and cognitive abilities. The engraved ochre pieces feature intricate geometric patterns, reflecting an appreciation for abstract design and possibly symbolic communication. The ability to create and interpret these symbols indicates a significant cognitive leap and a sophisticated understanding of representation and meaning

Engravings on various materials, such as bones, stones, and shells, further highlight the artistic and symbolic capabilities of early Homo sapiens. At sites like Blombos Cave, intricate geometric patterns have been found, indicating an appreciation for abstract design and possibly symbolic communication. These early artistic expressions reflect a cognitive ability to represent concepts and ideas symbolically, a trait that is a cornerstone of modern human behavior. Similar engravings have been found at other sites across Africa and Europe, suggesting that symbolic thought and artistic expression were widespread among early human populations. The ability to create such engravings required not only technical skill but also a cultural context that valued and understood symbolic representation.

Cave Paintings and Rock Art:

 As Homo sapiens migrated out of Africa and settled in various parts of the world, their artistic practices evolved. Some of the most significant early art comes from Europe, where cave paintings have been discovered dating back approximately 40,000 years. Sites like Chauvet and Lascaux in France, and Altamira in Spain, showcase stunning depictions of animals, human figures, and abstract symbols. These paintings were created using natural pigments such as ochre and charcoal, applied with brushes made from animal hair or even directly with the artists' hands.

 These cave paintings are not only aesthetically impressive but also reflect a deep understanding of the natural world and possibly spiritual beliefs. The choice of locations deep within caves, often in hard-to-reach areas, suggests that these artworks had special significance, possibly related to rituals or storytelling. The consistent themes and styles of these paintings across different sites indicate a shared cultural tradition and a sophisticated understanding of artistic techniques. The detailed and realistic representation of these animals suggests a deep understanding and observation of the natural world.

The creation of these cave paintings involved complex planning and execution. The artists used tools to apply the pigments, and the placement of the artworks deep within the caves indicates the use of artificial lighting, such as torches or lamps. This level of sophistication in the creation and placement of art reflects advanced cognitive abilities and social organization. The choice of locations deep within the caves, often in hard-to-reach areas, suggests that these paintings held special significance, possibly related to rituals or storytelling. The consistent themes and styles of these paintings across different sites indicate a shared cultural tradition and a sophisticated understanding of artistic techniques.

Symbolic Artifacts and Portable Art:

In addition to cave paintings, early humans created a variety of symbolic artifacts and portable art. Beads, pendants, and carved figurines have been found in archaeological sites across Africa, Europe, and Asia. These items were often made from materials such as bones, stones, and shells, and were used as jewelry or decorative objects. The crafting of these items required meticulous work and a high level of skill, reflecting the importance of symbolic behavior in early human societies.

The famous "Venus" figurines, which date back to around 25,000 years ago, are among the most well-known examples of prehistoric portable art. These small statuettes, often depicting voluptuous female figures, have been found across Europe and are believed to represent fertility or mother goddess figures. The widespread distribution of these figurines suggests that they played a significant role in the cultural and spiritual life of early humans. The crafting of these items required meticulous work and a high level of skill, reflecting the importance of symbolic behavior in early human societies.

In addition to beads, early humans created other symbolic artifacts such as carved figurines and decorated tools. These items often depicted animals or human figures and were likely used in rituals or as talismans. The discovery of these artifacts in various parts of the world indicates that symbolic thought and artistic expression were integral parts of early human culture. These objects not only served aesthetic purposes but also played a role in social and spiritual practices, helping to reinforce group identity and convey complex ideas and beliefs. The widespread use of these artifacts suggests a sophisticated understanding of symbolism and a capacity for abstract thinking.

Rituals and Early Religion:

The development of art and symbolic behavior was closely linked to the emergence of ritualistic practices and early forms of religion. Burial sites from this period often include grave goods such as tools, ornaments, and food, indicating beliefs in an afterlife and the importance of honoring the dead. The use of ochre in burials, often to decorate the body or grave, further highlights the symbolic significance of these rituals.

Sacred spaces, such as areas designated for burials or ritual activities, were also created during this time. These spaces reflect a sense of spirituality and a connection to the natural world. Early religious beliefs likely included the worship of natural elements, animals, and ancestors, as evidenced by the creation of symbolic artifacts associated with spiritual or ritualistic use.

The emergence of ritualistic behaviors and early forms of religion is evidenced by the burial of the dead with grave goods and the creation of sacred spaces. Burial practices during this period often included the placement of tools, ornaments, and other items with the deceased, indicating beliefs in an afterlife or the significance of the individual within the community. These practices reflect a growing complexity in social structures and a deepening sense of identity and community among early Homo sapiens.

Grave sites from this period often show evidence of careful preparation and the inclusion of items that were significant to the deceased. This suggests that early humans had developed complex beliefs about life and death, and that they engaged in rituals to honor and remember their dead. The presence of ochre in many burial sites, often used to decorate the body or grave, further indicates the symbolic importance of these rituals. Sacred spaces, such as areas designated for burials or ritual activities, were also created, reflecting a sense of spirituality and a connection to the natural world.

The development of early religious beliefs and practices is also evidenced by the creation of symbolic artifacts associated with spiritual or ritualistic use. For example, figurines and carvings depicting deities or spiritual beings have been found at various archaeological sites, suggesting that early humans believed in higher powers or spiritual forces. These artifacts provide insight into the early development of religious thought and the ways in which early Homo sapiens sought to understand and interact with the world around them.

Transition to Monumental Architecture:

As Homo sapiens transitioned from nomadic hunter-gatherer lifestyles to settled agricultural communities, their artistic and architectural achievements became more sophisticated. The construction of the first monumental structures began around 12,000 years ago, with sites like Göbekli Tepe in present-day Turkey. This site features massive stone pillars arranged in circular formations, decorated with intricate carvings of animals and abstract symbols. Göbekli Tepe is considered one of the earliest examples of large-scale architecture and organized labor, indicating a high level of social organization and cultural development.

The Neolithic period saw the rise of permanent settlements and the construction of complex societies. This era marked significant advancements in agriculture, technology, and social structures, paving the way for the development of early civilizations. The construction of large communal structures, such as temples and ceremonial centers, became increasingly common as human societies grew in complexity and size.

The First Pyramids:

The culmination of early human artistic and architectural endeavors is exemplified by the construction of the first pyramids in ancient Egypt. Around 4,700 years ago, the Egyptians began building these monumental structures as tombs for their pharaohs. The step pyramid of Djoser, constructed during the Third Dynasty by the architect Imhotep, is one of the earliest and most famous pyramids. This pyramid, made of limestone, features a series of stepped terraces that rise to a height of 62 meters.

The construction of the pyramids required advanced engineering skills, sophisticated knowledge of mathematics and astronomy, and a highly organized workforce. These monumental structures not only served as tombs but also as symbols of the pharaohs' divine authority and their connection to the gods. The pyramids stand as a testament to the artistic, technological, and cultural achievements of early human civilizations.

The evolution of Homo sapiens from their earliest expressions of art to the construction of the first pyramids reflects a remarkable journey of cognitive, cultural, and technological development. From the creation of symbolic artifacts and cave paintings to the rise of monumental architecture, early humans demonstrated an extraordinary capacity for creativity, organization, and expression. These advancements laid the foundation for the rich and diverse cultural traditions that characterize modern human civilization.

The early artistic expressions, such as the engraved ochre and shell beads from Blombos Cave, highlight the beginning of abstract thought and social communication through symbols. These initial steps in art and symbolism were not just about aesthetics but were deeply intertwined with social and cultural identities. As Homo sapiens migrated out of Africa, these practices evolved and spread, leading to the creation of elaborate cave paintings in Europe, which showcased a sophisticated understanding of the natural world and possibly spiritual beliefs.

Portable art and symbolic artifacts, including the famous Venus figurines, played crucial roles in social and ritualistic practices, indicating early forms of religious and spiritual beliefs. The burial practices and the creation of sacred spaces during this period further illustrate the growing complexity of social structures and the deepening sense of community and identity among early human groups.

The transition to settled agricultural communities brought about significant changes in artistic and architectural achievements. Sites like Göbekli Tepe represent the early stages of monumental architecture, reflecting advanced social organization and cultural development. This period marked the beginning of large-scale construction projects that required coordinated labor and sophisticated planning.

The construction of the first pyramids in ancient Egypt stands as a pinnacle of early human architectural and artistic achievements. These monumental structures symbolize the technological prowess, organizational capabilities, and spiritual beliefs of early civilizations. The pyramids were not just tombs but also served as enduring symbols of the pharaohs' divine authority and their connection to the gods.

Overall, the evolution of early art and symbolic behavior showcases the remarkable journey of Homo sapiens as they developed complex cognitive abilities, social structures, and cultural traditions. These advancements played a crucial role in shaping the trajectory of human history, leading to the development of the rich and diverse civilizations that we see today

CHAPTER 4:

OUR EMERGENCE OUT OF AFRICA

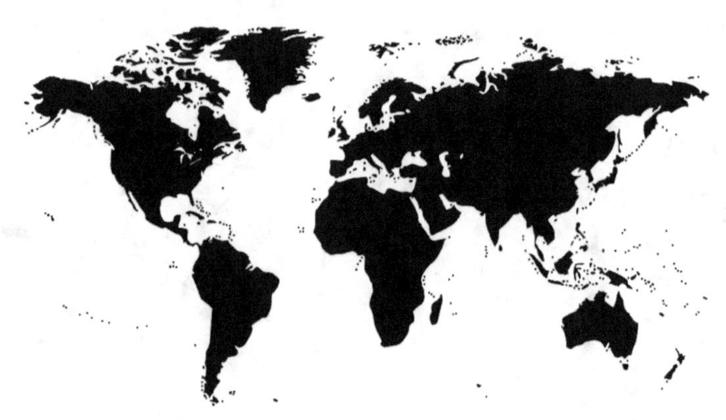

The migration of Homo sapiens out of Africa marks one of the most significant events in human history. This movement, spanning tens of thousands of years, saw early humans adapting to new environments, developing diverse cultures, and interacting with other hominin species. This chapter will explore the migration of Homo sapiens to each continent, detailing the reasons, methods, outcomes, and timeline of these remarkable journeys.

Middle East:

When and Where? (70,000 - 50,000 Years Ago)
The Middle East served as a crucial gateway for early humans migrating out of Africa. Around 60,000 to 50,000 years ago, Homo sapiens began to settle in the Levant region, which includes modern-day Jordan, Lebanon, and Syria. Archaeological sites such as Skhul and Qafzeh in the Levant provide some of the earliest evidence of modern humans in the region, dating back to around 100,000 years ago, although these early populations did not establish lasting settlements. The Middle East's strategic location made it a critical juncture for human migration, acting as a bridge between Africa and Eurasia. The region's varied terrain, including coastal plains, mountains, and river valleys, offered rich resources and a diverse range of habitats

How?

The successful settlement of Homo sapiens in the Middle East involved several key strategies. Early humans utilized natural shelters such as caves and rock overhangs to protect themselves from the elements. They developed advanced stone tools, including blades and points, which were used for hunting and processing food. These tools were often made from high-quality flint and other local stones, indicating a sophisticated understanding of materials and their properties. The use of fire for cooking and warmth was widespread, and they likely wore clothing made from animal hides to adapt to the varying climates of the region. Additionally, the strategic use of water sources, such as springs and rivers, was essential for sustaining larger populations. These technological and cultural adaptations were crucial for surviving in the diverse environments of the Middle East.

Why?

The migration into the Middle East was driven by a combination of factors, including climatic changes, population pressures, and the search for new resources. As the Sahara Desert expanded and contracted, it created corridors that facilitated migration. Additionally, the Middle East offered a rich and diverse environment with abundant water sources, plant life, and game animals, making it an attractive destination for early human populations seeking new territories and resources. The region's moderate climate and fertile lands were ideal for sustaining hunter-gatherer communities, allowing them to thrive and expand.

Immediate Results?

The immediate impact of Homo sapiens settling in the Middle East included interactions with other hominin species, particularly Neanderthals. Evidence of interbreeding between Homo sapiens and Neanderthals has been found in genetic studies, indicating that these populations not only coexisted but also exchanged genetic material. This genetic mixing contributed to the diversity of modern human populations. Additionally, the establishment of early human communities in the Middle East led to the development of new cultural practices and technologies, which would later spread to other regions. These innovations included more efficient hunting techniques, the creation of permanent shelters, and the establishment of complex social networks.

Later Results:

In the long term, the successful settlement of Homo sapiens in the Middle East set the stage for further migrations into Asia and Europe. The technological and cultural innovations developed in this region were carried by migrating populations, influencing the development of human societies in these areas. Additionally, the genetic legacy of interbreeding with Neanderthals has had a lasting impact on the genetic makeup of modern humans, contributing to genetic diversity and possibly influencing traits related to immune function and adaptation to different environments. The Middle East also became a center for early agriculture and urbanization, laying the groundwork for future civilizations.

Asia:

When and Where? (70,000 - 50,000 Years Ago)

From the Middle East, Homo sapiens expanded into Asia, reaching as far as India, Southeast Asia, and China. This migration began around 50,000 years ago and continued over millennia, with early humans moving along coastal routes and river valleys. Sites such as Niah Cave in Borneo, Liujiang in

China, and Lake Mungo in Australia provide evidence of early human presence in these regions by 40,000 years ago. The vast expanse of Asia, with its diverse climates and landscapes, presented both opportunities and challenges for early human settlers.

How?

 The migration into Asia involved several distinct routes and strategies. One of the primary routes was along the southern coastline of Asia, known as the "Southern Dispersal Route." This path took early humans from the Middle East, across the Arabian Peninsula, and along the coastal regions of South Asia. The presence of fertile river valleys, such as the Indus and Ganges, provided abundant resources and facilitated movement. Early humans utilized boats to navigate rivers and coastal waters, allowing them to explore and settle new areas. Additionally, the development of new tools and technologies, such as advanced stone tools and the use of fire for cooking and warmth, enabled them to adapt to the diverse environments of Asia.

Why?

 The migration into Asia was driven by several factors, including the search for new resources, population pressures, and climatic changes. As populations grew in the Middle East, groups of Homo sapiens began to explore new territories in search of food, water, and shelter. The diverse environments of Asia, from tropical rainforests to arid deserts and cold highlands, required adaptability and innovation. The push to explore new territories was also driven by the competition for resources within growing populations, as well as the attractive opportunities presented by the fertile lands and abundant resources found in various parts of Asia.

Immediate Results:

The immediate impact of Homo sapiens settling in Asia was the development of region-specific adaptations and cultures. In Southeast Asia, early humans adapted to tropical rainforests and coastal environments, developing tools and techniques for hunting and gathering in these ecosystems. In northern Asia, they faced colder climates, which led to the development of clothing, shelters, and hunting strategies suited to harsh conditions. Additionally, the interaction with Denisovans in parts of Asia contributed to the genetic diversity of modern populations, particularly in Melanesia and Aboriginal Australia.

Later Results?

Over time, the human populations in Asia diversified culturally and technologically. The development of agriculture around 10,000 years ago in the fertile valleys of the Yellow River and the Yangtze River in China marked a significant shift from hunter-gatherer societies to settled farming communities. This agricultural revolution led to the rise of early civilizations, characterized by complex social structures, written language, and technological advancements. The innovations and cultural practices developed in Asia had far-reaching impacts, influencing neighboring regions and laying the foundations for future empires and civilizations.

Europe:

When and Where? (45,000 - 35,000 Years Ago)

Homo sapiens began migrating into Europe around 45,000 years ago. This migration likely followed natural corridors such as the Danube River, which provided a pathway into Central and Western Europe. Early human presence in Europe is evidenced by archaeological sites like the Aurignacian culture in France and Germany, where sophisticated tools and symbolic artifacts have been discovered. The varied landscapes of Europe, including forests, mountains, and plains, presented new challenges and opportunities for early human settlers.

How?

The migration into Europe involved adapting to colder climates and diverse environments. Early humans developed specialized tools and clothing to survive the harsh winters of the Ice Age. They constructed shelters using available materials such as wood, animal hides, and mammoth bones. The use of fire for warmth and cooking became even more critical in the colder climates of Europe. Additionally, they hunted large Ice Age megafauna, such as mammoths and woolly rhinoceroses, using advanced hunting techniques and collaborative strategies.

Why?

The migration into Europe was driven by the search for new resources, population pressures, and the opportunities presented by the uninhabited or sparsely populated lands. The fertile river valleys, abundant game, and diverse plant life offered attractive opportunities for early human settlers. Additionally, the decline of Neanderthal populations in Europe created a vacuum that Homo sapiens were able to fill, further encouraging their expansion into the region.

Immediate Results:

The immediate impact of Homo sapiens settling in Europe included interactions with Neanderthals. Genetic evidence shows that interbreeding between Homo sapiens and

Neanderthals occurred, contributing to the genetic diversity of modern Europeans. This interaction was not just genetic but also cultural, as Homo sapiens adopted and improved upon some of the technologies and survival strategies of Neanderthals. The cultural innovations brought by Homo sapiens, such as advanced toolmaking techniques and artistic expressions, began to flourish. Sites like Chauvet and Lascaux in France, with their stunning cave paintings, reflect the sophisticated symbolic and artistic capabilities of these early humans. The establishment of permanent and semi-permanent settlements marked the beginning of more complex social structures and community organization. The initial adaptation to the European environment included the development of tailored clothing from animal hides and the construction of shelters using bones and hides, which were essential for surviving the harsh winters.

Later Results:

In the long term, the successful settlement of Homo sapiens in Europe led to the development of diverse cultures and technological advancements. The Upper Paleolithic period in Europe saw a flourishing of art and culture, with the creation of intricate Venus figurines and elaborate cave paintings. These artistic expressions indicate a rich symbolic and spiritual life. The development of more efficient hunting tools, such as the atlatl (spear-thrower), improved survival rates and allowed for greater exploitation of resources. The genetic legacy of interbreeding with Neanderthals has had a lasting impact on the genetic makeup of modern Europeans, contributing to traits related to immune function and adaptation to cold climates. Over time, these early Europeans developed complex social hierarchies and trade networks, leading to the formation of larger communities and eventually the establishment of agricultural societies and early urban centers.

Australia:

When and Where? (65,000 - 50,000 Years Ago)
 The colonization of Australia represents one of the earliest known instances of seafaring by Homo sapiens. Archaeological evidence from sites such as Madjedbebe in Northern Australia suggests that humans arrived as early as 65,000 years ago. These early settlers are believed to have crossed open waters from Southeast Asia using simple watercraft, indicating significant navigational skills and the ability to construct boats. The initial landings likely occurred in the northern regions of Australia, with subsequent migration spreading across the continent, reaching places like Lake Mungo in the south.

How?
 The migration to Australia required significant adaptations and innovations. Early humans likely used rafts or simple boats made from logs and reeds to navigate across the sea. Once on the continent, they adapted to the unique flora and fauna of Australia by developing specialized hunting techniques and tools. This included the use of boomerangs and spears for hunting large marsupials. The ability to create and manage fire was crucial for clearing land and driving game. Additionally, early Australians developed a deep understanding of the environment, which is reflected in their complex land management practices and use of resources. They created rock art and other symbolic artifacts, which provide insights into their rich cultural and spiritual life.

Why?

The migration to Australia was driven by a combination of environmental pressures, population growth, and the search for new resources. As human populations in Southeast Asia grew, groups began to explore new territories in search of food and living space. The rich and diverse ecosystems of Australia offered abundant resources, including game animals and edible plants. Additionally, the ability to navigate and settle new lands was likely driven by the human spirit of exploration and adaptability. The relatively stable climate and the presence of freshwater sources made Australia an attractive destination for these early explorers.

Immediate Results:

The immediate impact of settling in Australia included significant adaptations to the unique environment. Early Australians developed new tools and hunting strategies to capture large marsupials such as kangaroos and diprotodons. They also utilized fire for hunting and land management, creating a mosaic of habitats that supported diverse wildlife. The creation of rock art in places like Arnhem Land and the Kimberley region indicates a rich cultural and spiritual life. These early artworks often depict animals, human figures, and symbolic designs, reflecting the importance of storytelling and ritual in their societies. The establishment of stable communities allowed for the development of complex social structures and cultural traditions.

Later Results:

Over time, the Aboriginal cultures that developed in Australia became some of the oldest continuous cultures in the world.

These communities maintained a profound connection to the land and its history, passing down knowledge through oral traditions, art, and ritual practices. The development of complex social networks and trade routes facilitated the exchange of goods and ideas across vast distances. The sustainable land management practices of early Australians, including the use of controlled burns, helped maintain biodiversity and ecological balance. These practices continue to influence modern conservation efforts. Additionally, the rich cultural heritage of Aboriginal Australians, including their art, music, and storytelling, remains a vital part of the global cultural landscape.

The Americas:

When and Where? (20,000 - 15,000 Years Ago)

The Americas were among the last continents to be colonized by Homo sapiens. The prevailing theory suggests that humans migrated from Siberia to North America via the Bering Land Bridge during the Last Glacial Maximum, around 20,000 to 15,000 years ago. This land bridge, known as Beringia, connected Asia and North America during periods of lower sea levels. Archaeological evidence from sites such as Bluefish Caves in Canada and Monte Verde in Chile indicates that early humans had spread throughout North and South America by around 14,000 years ago. Notably, Homo sapiens are the only Homo species known to have reached the Americas and Australia, marking a significant achievement in human migration and adaptation.

How:

The migration into the Americas involved several stages and

routes. Early humans likely followed herds of megafauna across the Bering Land Bridge into Alaska. From there, they spread southward along the western coastlines and through ice-free corridors in the interior of North America. The development of new hunting technologies, such as Clovis points, allowed early Americans to effectively hunt large game, including mammoths and mastodons. Additionally, the use of atlatls and other advanced tools enabled them to adapt to a wide range of environments, from the Arctic tundra to the temperate forests and deserts of the Americas. The ability to construct shelters and manage fire was essential for surviving the diverse climates they encountered.

Why:

 The migration into the Americas was driven by several factors, including climatic changes, population pressures, and the pursuit of new resources. As ice sheets retreated and sea levels fell during the Last Glacial Maximum, new land became accessible, prompting human groups to explore these areas. The rich and varied ecosystems of the Americas offered abundant resources, including large game animals and diverse plant life. Additionally, the drive for exploration and the adaptability of Homo sapiens played a crucial role in their successful colonization of these new territories. The Americas presented opportunities for new hunting grounds, fertile lands, and habitable regions that could support growing human populations.

Immediate Results:

 The immediate impact of human settlement in the Americas included significant ecological and cultural changes. Early human populations adapted to the local environments by developing specialized tools and hunting strategies. The widespread use of Clovis points, for example, revolutionized hunting practices and allowed for the efficient capture of large game. The establishment of early communities led to the development of diverse cultures, each with its own unique adaptations and traditions. The creation of rock art, carvings, and other symbolic artifacts indicates a rich cultural and spiritual life. Additionally, the arrival of humans in the Americas coincided with the decline and extinction of many large mammal species, possibly due to overhunting and environmental changes.

Later Results:

Over time, the diverse cultures and societies that developed in the Americas laid the foundation for complex civilizations. The transition from hunter-gatherer lifestyles to settled agricultural communities began around 10,000 years ago, with the domestication of plants such as maize, beans, and squash. This agricultural revolution led to the rise of early civilizations, such as the Olmec, Maya, and Inca, which built impressive cities, developed writing systems, and created advanced technologies. The cultural and technological achievements of these civilizations continue to influence modern societies. Additionally, the genetic legacy of the initial human populations in the Americas is evident in the diverse indigenous cultures that thrive today, preserving rich traditions and knowledge.

Conclusion:

The migration of Homo sapiens out of Africa and their subsequent colonization of the globe is a testament to human adaptability, ingenuity, and resilience. Each continent presented unique challenges and opportunities, shaping the cultural and technological evolution of human societies. From the early artistic expressions in Africa and Europe to the monumental achievements of the first pyramids, the journey of Homo sapiens reflects a continuous thread of innovation, adaptation, and cultural richness that continues to define humanity today. The genetic and cultural legacies of these migrations have left an indelible mark on the history of our species, demonstrating the remarkable ability of humans to thrive in diverse environments and create complex, vibrant societies.

CHAPTER 5:
THE PRO HUNTERS PERIOD

The Pro Hunters Period, spanning from around 20,000 to 15,000 years ago, marks a pinnacle in the evolution of human hunting techniques and technology. This era, situated just before the advent of agriculture, showcases the height of hunting sophistication in prehistoric Europe. The name "Pro Hunters Period" reflects the advanced skills and innovations in hunting that characterized this time, laying the foundation for the subsequent agricultural revolution, which would eventually shift the focus from hunting to farming. This chapter delves into the intricacies of hunting practices during this period, including the tools used, the techniques employed, and the variety of prey targeted by early Europeans.

Advanced Hunting Tools:

The bow and arrow were among the most significant technological advancements of this period. This tool allowed hunters to strike from a distance with remarkable accuracy and lethality. Bows were typically made from flexible woods such as yew or ash, while arrows were crafted from lighter woods and tipped with finely worked flint or bone points. Feathers were attached to the ends of arrows to stabilize their flight, showcasing an advanced understanding of aerodynamics. This innovation significantly enhanced hunting efficiency, enabling hunters to target prey from safer distances and increasing their success rates in capturing fast-moving animals. The precision and effectiveness of the bow and arrow made it a revolutionary tool in the arsenal of early humans, allowing them to hunt more stealthily and with greater success.

The atlatl, or spear-thrower, was another crucial tool during this period. It extended the thrower's arm, providing leverage to hurl spears with greater force and precision over longer distances. This increased range and power made the atlatl especially useful for hunting large game, such as reindeer and bison, from a safer distance. The use of the atlatl is evidenced by finds of spear points and atlatl weights at various archaeological sites across Europe. This technology represented a significant advancement in hunting efficiency, allowing early humans to engage larger and more dangerous animals with reduced risk. The development and use of the atlatl demonstrate the ingenuity and adaptability of early human societies, as they continuously sought ways to improve their hunting capabilities and enhance their survival strategies.

Spears remained a fundamental part of the hunting arsenal. These tools, often tipped with meticulously crafted stone or bone points, were used both for thrusting at close range and for throwing. The development of lighter, more aerodynamic throwing spears increased their effectiveness. Lances, which were longer and heavier, were primarily used for thrusting and were particularly useful for large game hunts. The refinement of spear technology, including the use of hafting techniques to attach stone points securely to wooden shafts, exemplifies the technological ingenuity of early humans during this period. These advancements in spear technology allowed for more efficient hunting of large game, ensuring a more reliable food supply and contributing to the overall success and stability of early human communities.

Blade technology also saw significant advancements during the

Pro Hunters Period. Long, thin stone blades were used to produce a variety of specialized tools, including knives, scrapers, and projectile points. These blades were often hafted onto wooden or bone handles, making them more versatile and efficient. The intricate flintknapping techniques used to produce these blades demonstrate a high level of craftsmanship and understanding of lithic materials. The development of blade technology not only improved hunting efficiency but also facilitated the processing of animal hides and meat, supporting other aspects of survival. These specialized tools allowed early humans to effectively butcher and process game, ensuring that no part of the animal was wasted and providing essential resources for clothing, shelter, and toolmaking.

Hunting Techniques:

 Group hunting was a common practice during the Pro Hunters Period. This strategy was particularly important for taking down large game animals. Groups of hunters would work together to drive herds of animals into natural traps, such as gorges or ravines, where they could be more easily killed. This method required sophisticated planning and communication, highlighting the social and cooperative nature of early human communities. The coordination and teamwork involved in group hunting not only increased the success rate of hunts but also reinforced social bonds and communal living. The ability to plan and execute complex hunting strategies reflects the advanced cognitive abilities and social structures of these early human societies, demonstrating their capacity for collaboration and collective problem-solving.

Ambush hunting was another effective technique, where hunters would hide and wait for animals to come close before launching a surprise attack. This method was effective for both large and small game and relied on the hunters' knowledge of animal behavior and movement patterns. Natural features like waterholes or game trails were often used as ambush sites. The ability to patiently wait and strategically place hunters to maximize the chances of a successful kill indicates a deep understanding of the natural world and animal behavior. This technique required careful observation and intimate knowledge of the habits and habitats of prey animals, showcasing the deep ecological knowledge possessed by early humans.

The use of fire was also strategically employed in hunting. Controlled burns would clear underbrush and create open areas that made it easier to spot and pursue game. Additionally, fire was used to harden wooden spear points, making them more durable and effective for hunting. The controlled use of fire not only improved hunting efficiency but also played a role in landscape management, creating habitats that supported a diversity of game animals. This understanding of fire management reflects a sophisticated level of ecological knowledge and manipulation.

Targeted Prey:

During the Pro Hunters Period, large game animals were the primary targets. These included mammoths, woolly rhinoceroses, reindeer, horses, and bison. Hunting these massive creatures required significant skill and teamwork, as well as the use of robust and effective tools. The meat from these animals provided a substantial food source, while their hides were used for clothing and shelter, and their bones for tools and fuel. The ability to successfully hunt such large animals indicates a high level of physical and technological prowess. These large game hunts were often central to the survival and prosperity of early human communities, providing essential resources and opportunities for social and cultural activities centered around the hunt.

In addition to large game, smaller animals were also hunted. This included rabbits, hares, birds, and fish. Small game was typically caught using traps, snares, and nets, which were strategically placed along animal trails or near water sources. The diversification of hunting strategies to include smaller game ensured a more stable and varied food supply. The development of specialized tools for small game hunting, such as fishhooks and bird snares, demonstrates the adaptability and resourcefulness of early humans. The ability to effectively hunt and trap small game allowed for a more balanced diet and reduced the risk of food shortages, especially during times when large game was scarce or migratory patterns changed.

Seasonal hunting played a crucial role in the survival strategies of early humans. Early humans were adept at following the migratory patterns of their prey. Seasonal hunting allowed them to exploit the movements of animals, such as reindeer, that migrated to different areas throughout the year. This practice required extensive knowledge of the landscape and animal behavior, as well as the ability to travel long distances to follow the herds. The ability to predict and follow seasonal migrations highlights the advanced planning and logistical capabilities of these early communities. Seasonal hunting ensured that early humans could take advantage of the abundance of game at different times of the year, providing a consistent food supply and supporting the growth and stability of their populations.

Social and Cultural Aspects:

The development of specialized tools for hunting, butchering, and processing game indicates a high level of technological advancement. Different tools were crafted for specific purposes, such as skinning knives, scrapers for cleaning hides, and needles for sewing garments from animal skins. This specialization reflects a deep understanding of materials and their uses, as well as the ability to innovate and improve upon existing technologies. The variety and complexity of tools found at archaeological sites from this period demonstrate the sophisticated craftsmanship and technological ingenuity of early humans. These advancements in toolmaking not only improved hunting efficiency but also supported other aspects of survival, such as clothing production, shelter construction, and food processing.

Hunting played a central role in the cultural and spiritual life of early Europeans. This is evident in the extensive rock art and carvings from this period, which often depict hunting scenes and animals. Sites like Chauvet and Lascaux in France showcase elaborate cave paintings that highlight the importance of hunting in daily life and spiritual practices. These artworks not only served as a form of expression but also likely played a role in rituals and the transmission of knowledge. The depiction of hunting scenes in art suggests that hunting was deeply embedded in the social and cultural identity of these communities. The presence of hunting-related symbols and motifs in art indicates that hunting was not only a practical activity but also a significant cultural and spiritual practice, reflecting the deep connection between early humans and their environment.

The need for coordinated hunting efforts likely led to the development of more complex social structures. Roles and responsibilities within hunting groups were likely divided based on skills and experience, fostering cooperation and social cohesion. This organization was crucial for successful hunts and the overall survival of the community. The social dynamics of hunting groups, including leadership roles and communal sharing of resources, contributed to the development of early forms of social organization and governance. The cooperative nature of hunting activities helped to strengthen social bonds and build a sense of community, laying the foundation for more complex social structures and interactions.

The Pro Hunters Period represents a time of remarkable innovation and adaptation in human history. The evolution of hunting tools and techniques allowed Homo sapiens to effectively exploit their environments and secure a stable food supply. During this era, the refinement of the bow and arrow significantly increased hunting efficiency, allowing for greater accuracy and safety in targeting prey from a distance. The sophisticated use of atlatls, which extended the thrower's arm to provide greater leverage and force for hurling spears, enabled early humans to hunt larger game with reduced risk. The development of specialized blades and composite tools, crafted with precision from stone and bone, enhanced the overall effectiveness of hunting and processing game. By the end of this period, around 15,000 years ago, humans had become highly skilled hunters, capable of taking down a wide range of game using diverse tools and strategies. These advancements laid the foundation for the eventual transition to settled agricultural societies and the rise of early civilizations. The ingenuity and adaptability displayed during the Pro Hunters Period continue to be a testament to the resourcefulness and resilience of early Homo sapiens, highlighting the dynamic nature of human evolution and cultural development.

CHAPTER 6:

STORY: BOUND BY HOOFBEATS

This story is a work of imagination, and while the names and exact language may not be historically accurate, the events, tools, and techniques described are based on realistic historical contexts. The goal of this chapter is to provide an engaging narrative that is both educational and enjoyable. Now, let's begin our journey into the life of two hunters 15,000 years ago in the area now known as the London Borough of Enfield.

London Borough of Enfield, UK, 13,232 BCE

It is 6 AM, the sky is clear, and the stars are still visible. Emma is sitting near a river, relaxing. The river flows gently, its surface shimmering with the reflections of the fading stars. The surrounding area is lush with greenery, and the sound of water creates a soothing backdrop. Standing at 5'7" and weighing 125 pounds, with blue eyes and straight brown short hair, she is 33 years old. She looks at the sky as the stars begin to vanish, wondering what they are. Suddenly, she hears a familiar voice: "You woke up early again. Do you have sleep problems?" Emma replies, "No, I'm feeling alright, even better actually. What about you, Rayan?"

Rayan, standing at 6'2" and weighing 180 pounds, with brown eyes and straight black hair, is 20 years old. While Emma possesses the skills, experience, and confidence of many years, Rayan is known for his strength and good judgment. He answers with a small smile, "I'm okay," and joins her by the river. For an hour, they enjoy the tranquility of the early morning, their camaraderie evident in the quiet ease of their conversation. They talk about the day ahead, share memories of past hunts, and occasionally fall into a comfortable silence, simply enjoying the peaceful sounds of nature around them. The river flows gently beside them, birds begin to chirp as the forest wakes up, and the sunlight gradually warms the cool morning air. Their bond is strengthened by these moments of shared stillness and connection.

As the sun rises, they decide to return to their group of 36 people. Emma heads straight to the toolmaker to check if her bow and arrows are ready. The toolmaker, skilled in his craft, tells her to wait another 15 minutes. Meanwhile, Rayan is eating a freshly caught rabbit from the previous day's hunt. Emma, after receiving her meticulously crafted bow and arrows, approaches Rayan. "Want to go hunt some horses?" she asks, her eyes glinting with excitement. Rayan responds, "Don't we have enough food for the month?" Emma, grabbing his hand and pulling him up, smiles playfully, "Come on, it will be fun." Rayan, unable to resist her enthusiasm, sighs and agrees, "Huh, sure."

Part 2: The Journey Begins:

Rayan grabbed his bow and arrows while Emma said, "Did you see the two horses the group hunted yesterday?" Rayan replied, "Yes, and that's why maybe we shouldn't go." Emma countered, "Maybe you're right, but like I said, it will be fun." Rayan, with a reluctant smile, answered, "Okay, I'm ready. Let's go."

As they set off, the earth shifted slightly beneath their feet, causing a momentary imbalance. Rayan looked around with a puzzled expression and asked, "What is this?" Emma, maintaining her calm demeanor, responded, "It's a light earthquake." Rayan, curious and slightly concerned, inquired further, "What causes it?" Emma recalled a conversation and explained, "Florence said that the mountains express their love for each other by shaking the earth." Rayan, raising an eyebrow skeptically, asked, "And you believe Florence, really?" Emma laughed, a melodic sound that lightened the mood, "I know she seems odd sometimes... okay, most of the time, but it's the only explanation I found, and I think it's romantic, something you should try sometimes." Rayan chuckled, his skepticism fading, "Is shaking the earth more romantic than a flower?" Emma, with a playful glint in her eye, replied, "Okay, I guess not."

They continued their journey, the landscape around them gradually changing from the soft greens of the riverside to the more rugged terrain of the open plains. The morning sun cast long shadows, warming the cool earth beneath their feet. Birds chirped in the trees, and the occasional rustle of leaves indicated the presence of small animals. Their path took them through dense woodlands, where the canopy overhead filtered the sunlight, creating a dappled pattern on the ground. The air was fresh, filled with the earthy scent of damp leaves and the occasional whiff of wildflowers.

Eventually, they reached a hill that offered a panoramic view of the surrounding area. The hunters often used this vantage point to scout for prey. From the top, the world spread out before them like a vast, living map. Fields of wild grasses swayed gently in the breeze, and the distant outline of the forest framed the horizon. As they scanned the landscape, they spotted a small pack of horses grazing peacefully in the distance. Emma's face lit up with excitement, her eyes sparkling with anticipation. "Let's go," she said, her voice filled with eagerness and determination.

Part 3: The Hunt

They descended the hill, heading toward the pack of horses while preparing their weapons. As they reached the herd, Emma signaled which horse they would target. She took the lead with Rayan just behind her. Emma aimed for a young horse, her movements slow and deliberate to avoid startling the herd. Rayan, positioned right behind her, whispered, "I'm ready." Without hesitation, Emma released her arrow, striking the horse in the chest. The horse reared up briefly before collapsing. Rayan immediately followed with a precise shot to the neck, ensuring the horse was swiftly brought down.

Emma knelt beside the horse's body, her face lighting up with a satisfied smile. "I told you it would be fun," she said. Rayan nodded and replied, "I'll get the drag wood. Stay here." The drag wood, a simple yet effective tool for carrying heavy loads, was kept on the hill they had scouted earlier. Rayan quickly returned with it, and together they placed the horse onto the drag wood. They moved quickly and efficiently, knowing they had to hurry back to their group before any wild animals were drawn to the scent of fresh blood.

The journey back to camp was brisk, the weight of their prize making the trek challenging but rewarding. They reached home, greeted by the appreciative smiles of their community. Emma and Rayan handed the horse over to two women specialized in cutting and stripping animals. The women, with expert hands, began their work immediately. Meanwhile, Emma and Rayan started a fire. Once the horse was processed, Emma returned to the women and grabbed some meat.

Part 4: The Attack

The first light of dawn had barely begun to break over the horizon when Emma and Rayan were jolted awake by the sounds of chaos. Although most nights Emma and Rayan slept in the same tent, this time they hadn't. The camp was under attack. Another group, fierce and desperate, had descended upon them. The air was filled with shouts, cries, and the clash of weapons.

Emma sprang to her feet, grabbing her bow and arrows. She moved swiftly through the camp, her heart pounding as she saw members of her group being overwhelmed. She fired arrows with deadly accuracy, each shot taking down one of the attackers. Despite her efforts, the enemy was too numerous. They had already killed most of her group, their bodies strewn across the camp in a scene of utter devastation.

Emma fought with all her strength, but she was soon surrounded. Her bow was knocked from her hands, and she found herself facing three attackers. They overpowered her, forcing her to the ground while one of them was about to cut her clothes. Just as this attacker raised his knife, a loud cry echoed through the chaos.

Rayan, covered in blood and filled with fierce determination, charged at the attackers. He moved with the fury of a cornered beast, striking down two of the men with swift, brutal efficiency. The third attacker turned to face him, but Rayan was relentless, delivering a final, deadly blow with his bare hands, punching him repeatedly. It wasn't until Emma, regaining her composure, pulled Rayan away that he stopped.

Breathing heavily, Rayan turned to Emma, who was battered but alive. "We need to go, now!" he urged, grabbing her hand. Emma, dazed but determined, nodded. They fled the camp, running towards the forest. The dense trees provided cover, and they moved as quickly and quietly as they could, the sounds of the battle fading behind them.

They ran until they could run no more, finally stopping to catch their breath. Emma looked at Rayan, her eyes filled with a burning resolve. "I will make them pay for this," she whispered, her voice strong despite the turmoil they had just escaped. Rayan nodded, his expression grim. "We need to keep moving. We can't stay here," he said, his voice steady despite the turmoil they had just escaped.

Together, they ventured deeper into the forest, seeking refuge and safety. The loss of their group weighed heavily on them, but they knew they had to survive. Emma and Rayan, bound by the horrors they had endured and the strength they had found in each other, moved forward into the unknown, determined to rebuild and continue their journey.

Part 5: The Return

Emma and Rayan found an empty cave, its entrance partially

hidden by thick foliage. Inside, the cave was dry and spacious enough for them to rest. Rayan immediately began tending to Emma's wounds, using herbs and clean strips of cloth they had brought with them. "We need to decide what to do next," Emma said, wincing slightly as Rayan applied a poultice to a cut on her arm. "I want to go back. I'm sure there are still survivors."

Rayan shook his head, his expression resolute. "We should get away from here. Maybe we'll find another group."

Emma's eyes blazed with determination. "You saw what those men were about to do to me. There will still be women alive. I'm going back with or without you."

Rayan sighed, looking torn. "First, get some sleep. We'll see." Emma shook her head. "I can't. What if it happens again? We need to strike tonight."

As night fell, they prepared to leave the cave. On their way, they encountered a few members of their group who had been on a hunting trip. Relief washed over Emma and Rayan as they shared what had happened. The hunters, horrified and angered by the news, agreed to join them in the attack and provided Emma and Rayan with additional weapons.

Under the cover of darkness, the group made their way back to the camp. The element of surprise was on their side. They moved silently, their faces set with grim determination. As they approached the enemy camp, Emma felt a surge of adrenaline. This was their chance to reclaim their home and rescue any survivors.

The attack was swift and brutal. Emma fought fiercely, her skills and determination driving her forward. Rayan stayed close, ensuring no harm came to her. They struck with precision, taking down several attackers before they even realized what was happening.

In the midst of the chaos, Emma spotted a group of women being held captive. She rushed towards them, freeing them from their bonds. Just as she turned to help another captive, she felt a sharp pain in her side. She looked down to see a spear protruding from her body. The world around her began to blur, and she collapsed to the ground.

Rayan, seeing Emma fall, stopped fighting and rushed back to Emma, who was struggling to fend off her attackers. He stayed by her side while others continued to fight. Rayan cradled Emma in his arms.

"Emma, stay with me," he pleaded, tears streaming down his face. But Emma's eyes were already losing their light. She managed a weak smile, her hand reaching up to touch his face. "I told you it would be fun," she whispered, her voice barely audible. She kissed him on the cheek before her strength faded away.

With those final words, Emma's hand fell limp, and her eyes closed for the last time. Emma lost her life, and Rayan lost his purpose. He continued to cry as the sounds of screaming filled the place.

As morning broke, the fight was finally over, and the group had taken back their home. Rayan remained with Emma, burying her with care and gently placing flowers on her grave. He whispered something softly, then stood up and walked away.

 He grabbed a bow and arrow and headed toward the forest. A member of the group asked, "Where are you going?" Rayan replied, "Hunting horses. It will be fun." With those words, Rayan vanished into the forest, the trees swallowing him up, and he was never seen again.

CHAPTER 7:
THE BEGINNINGS OF ANIMAL DOMESTICATION

The Dawn of Domestication:

The domestication of animals marked a pivotal transformation in human history, signaling the shift from nomadic lifestyles to settled agricultural societies. This momentous change began around 10,000 to 15,000 years ago during the Neolithic Revolution, a period of significant technological and societal advancement. The earliest evidence of animal domestication is traced back to the Fertile Crescent, a region in the Middle East that includes modern-day Iraq, Syria, Lebanon, Jordan, and parts of Turkey, Iran and other places. This area, renowned for its fertile land and conducive climate, provided the perfect conditions for early humans to begin cultivating plants and taming animals.

The domestication of animals was not an overnight development but rather a gradual process that unfolded over millennia. Early humans began to recognize the advantages of keeping animals close, not just for the immediate benefits of meat and hides but also for their potential as a sustainable resource for milk, wool, labor, and companionship. This symbiotic relationship evolved through mutual adaptation, with humans learning to manage and breed animals while animals became increasingly accustomed to human presence and care.

Motivations for Domestication:

The motivation behind domestication was driven by the need for a stable and reliable food source. As human populations grew and hunting alone could no longer sustain communities, the taming and breeding of animals offered a consistent supply of meat, milk, and eggs. This reliability reduced the uncertainty and dangers associated with hunting, allowing for more secure and predictable food resources. Additionally, the presence of domesticated animals enabled early humans to settle in one place, leading to the establishment of permanent villages and the development of more complex societal structures.

Domesticated animals also provided labor, which was a significant factor in the development of agriculture. Animals such as oxen and donkeys were used for plowing fields and transporting goods, greatly enhancing agricultural productivity and allowing humans to cultivate larger areas of land. The use of animal labor was a revolutionary development, making it possible to sustain larger populations and complex societies.

Protection and hunting were also crucial motivations for domestication. Early humans recognized that certain animals could assist in hunting and provide protection from predators and rival groups. Dogs, for instance, were among the first animals domesticated, initially aiding in hunting by tracking and retrieving game. Over time, they also became protectors of human settlements, alerting their owners to potential threats and defending against intruders. This dual role made dogs invaluable companions in the early stages of human society, providing both practical and emotional support.

The First Domesticated Animals:

One of the first animals to be domesticated was the dog, with evidence suggesting this relationship began around 15,000 years ago in Eurasia. some dated to even 30000 years ago.

Initially, wolves may have started scavenging near human settlements, and over time, a mutually beneficial relationship developed. Humans provided food and protection, while dogs offered their keen senses and hunting skills. This companionship evolved, with dogs becoming protectors and helpers in various human endeavors.

Sheep and goats followed as some of the earliest domesticated livestock, around 10,000 years ago in the Fertile Crescent. These animals were prized for their meat, milk, wool, and hides. Their relatively docile nature made them suitable for herding, and they could thrive in the varied climates of the region. The domestication of sheep and goats represented a significant step in human society, providing reliable sources of food and materials that could be stored and traded.

The Domestication of Cattle and Pigs:

Cattle domestication began around 8,000 years ago in the Near East and parts of Africa. These large animals provided not only meat and milk but also labor. Cattle were used to plow fields and transport goods, playing a crucial role in agricultural societies. The ability to use cattle for labor transformed agriculture, allowing for the cultivation of larger plots of land and increasing food production.

Pigs were domesticated around 9,000 years ago in the Near East and China. Unlike cattle and sheep, pigs were primarily valued for their meat. They were versatile animals, capable of thriving in various environments, and they had a rapid growth rate, making them an efficient source of protein. Pigs were often kept near human settlements, where they could forage and recycle waste, providing a practical and sustainable food source.

The Role of Cats in Early Societies:

Cats were domesticated around 9,500 years ago, with some of the earliest evidence coming from a Neolithic site in Cyprus. These cats were likely attracted to human settlements by the abundance of rodents, which were drawn to stored grain. This relationship was mutually beneficial: humans gained a natural form of pest control, while cats had a steady food source.

In ancient Egypt, cats were revered and often associated with deities like Bastet. They played an important role in both practical and spiritual aspects of Egyptian life. Cats were kept in homes and temples, and harming a cat was considered a grave offense. This reverence spread from Egypt to other parts of the world, and cats became cherished members of households, admired for their independence, grace, and ability to keep pests at bay.

The impact of animal domestication on human societies was profound. It allowed for more stable and reliable food sources, which in turn supported population growth and the development of complex societies. The ability to settle in one place led to the establishment of permanent villages and the rise of agriculture. Domesticated animals provided labor, transportation, and materials, further enhancing human capabilities and enabling the development of trade networks and economic systems.

The symbiotic relationship between humans and domesticated animals continues to shape our world today. From the food we eat to the clothes we wear and the tools we use, the legacy of animal domestication is evident in every aspect of our lives. Horses, too, domesticated around 5,500 years ago on the steppes of Central Asia, have had a profound impact on human history, revolutionizing transportation, agriculture, and warfare. This chapter in human history is a testament to the ingenuity and adaptability of our species, demonstrating our ability to transform the natural world to meet our needs and improve our quality of life.

CHAPTER 8:
THE START OF AGRICULTURE

Origins of Agriculture:

 The advent of agriculture was the most transformative event in human history, marking the transition from nomadic hunter-gatherer societies to settled agricultural communities. This monumental shift, often referred to as the Neolithic Revolution, began around 10,000 years ago and laid the foundation for the development of civilization as we know it. This period was characterized by significant advancements in human technology and lifestyle, with agriculture likely beginning independently in several regions around the world. One of the earliest and most significant areas was the Fertile Crescent in the Middle East, encompassing parts of modern-day Iraq, Syria, Lebanon, Israel, Jordan, and Turkey. The Fertile Crescent, with its rich and fertile land, offered ideal conditions for the cultivation of wild grains and legumes, allowing early humans to experiment with and eventually develop agricultural practices.

 Archaeological evidence suggests that people in this region began cultivating plants and domesticating animals around 10,000 BCE. One of the first plants to be domesticated was wheat, originally a wild grass. Early farmers selected seeds from the most productive plants, gradually enhancing their yield and hardiness through a process known as artificial selection. This method led to the development of domesticated wheat varieties that could be reliably harvested and stored. Alongside wheat, barley, lentils, chickpeas, peas, and flax were also among the first crops to be cultivated in the Fertile Crescent. These early agricultural practices were essential in transforming human societies, enabling them to settle in one place and support larger populations.

The Process of Domestication:

The process of plant domestication involved several key steps, each contributing to the gradual shift from wild foraging to controlled agriculture. Initially, early humans collected wild plants and observed which ones had desirable traits, such as larger seeds or tastier fruits. They began to cultivate these plants intentionally, planting seeds in plots of land they had cleared of competing vegetation. Over generations, through a process of selective breeding, these plants became more productive and less dependent on natural conditions, thus becoming domesticated. The ability to control the growth and harvest of these plants marked a significant leap in human ingenuity, leading to a more stable and reliable food source.

The domestication of animals often followed a similar pattern. Early humans started by capturing wild animals and keeping them in captivity, where they could control their breeding and diet. They selected animals that were docile, easy to manage, and productive in terms of meat, milk, or labor. Over time, these animals adapted to living with humans, leading to the domesticated species we are familiar with today. This symbiotic relationship between humans and animals was crucial in the development of early agricultural societies, providing not only food but also labor and companionship.

Early Agricultural Practices:

Early agricultural practices were labor-intensive and required significant adaptation and innovation. In the Fertile Crescent, early farmers developed techniques such as irrigation, plowing, and crop rotation to improve agricultural productivity. Irrigation allowed them to control the water supply, ensuring crops received enough moisture even during dry periods. This advancement enabled the cultivation of crops in regions that would otherwise be unsuitable for farming. Plowing, initially done by hand and later with the help of animals, made it easier to prepare the soil for planting, increasing the efficiency and yield of agricultural endeavors. Crop rotation helped maintain soil fertility by alternating the types of crops grown in a particular field, preventing nutrient depletion and reducing the likelihood of pest infestations.

Agriculture also led to the development of new tools and technologies. Early farmers invented sickles for harvesting grain, grinding stones for processing it into flour, and pottery for storing surplus food. These innovations not only made farming more efficient but also facilitated the storage and distribution of food, which was essential for supporting larger, more complex societies. The ability to store surplus food allowed communities to survive periods of scarcity and laid the groundwork for trade and economic development.

The Impact on Human Societies:

The shift to agriculture had profound impacts on human societies, fundamentally altering their structure and dynamics. One of the most significant changes was the establishment of permanent settlements. As people began to rely on cultivated crops and domesticated animals for their food, they no longer needed to move constantly in search of resources. This sedentary lifestyle led to the development of villages and eventually cities, where people could live year-round. Permanent settlements allowed for the accumulation of surplus food, which in turn enabled population growth and the specialization of labor. With a stable food supply, not everyone needed to be involved in food production. This freed up individuals to pursue other activities, such as crafting tools, building infrastructure, and developing trade. The specialization of labor led to the emergence of new professions and social hierarchies, laying the groundwork for complex societies and the development of civilization.

Agriculture also had significant environmental impacts. The clearing of land for farming altered natural landscapes, and irrigation systems changed the flow of rivers and streams. The domestication of plants and animals led to the creation of new ecosystems, where domesticated species thrived under human care. These changes often resulted in increased biodiversity in some areas but also caused the decline of wild species and natural habitats in others. The environmental transformations brought about by agriculture were profound, reshaping entire regions and influencing the development of human societies.

The Spread of Agriculture:

The practice of agriculture spread from the Fertile Crescent to other parts of the world, driven by the movement of people, ideas, and technologies. As agricultural techniques were shared and adapted to different environments, new centers of agriculture emerged. In East Asia, rice and millet became staple crops, while in the Americas, maize, beans, and squash were cultivated. In Africa, sorghum and yams were domesticated, along with the development of cattle herding. Each region developed its own unique agricultural practices and crop varieties, contributing to the diversity of global agriculture. The exchange of agricultural knowledge and products between regions through trade and migration further accelerated the spread of agriculture and the development of interconnected societies.

The global spread of agriculture facilitated cultural exchanges and the diffusion of innovations, leading to the rise of trade networks and economic systems. These interactions between different agricultural societies contributed to the development of more sophisticated technologies and social structures, fostering the growth of early civilizations. The diffusion of agricultural practices and crops across continents played a crucial role in shaping the cultural and economic landscapes of ancient human societies.

The Role of Agriculture in the Rise of Civilization:

Agriculture played a crucial role in the rise of civilization. The ability to produce surplus food allowed for the growth of larger, more complex societies with specialized labor and social hierarchies. Permanent settlements became centers of culture, politics, and economy, leading to the development of early cities and states. The surplus food produced by agricultural societies supported the creation of monumental architecture, the development of writing and record-keeping, and the establishment of trade networks that connected distant regions. The stability provided by agriculture also enabled the development of laws, governance structures, and organized religions. As societies grew larger and more complex, they required new forms of social organization and cooperation. The surplus resources generated by agriculture provided the means to support these developments, leading to the rise of powerful empires and sophisticated cultures.

The agricultural revolution transformed human societies, creating the conditions necessary for the development of complex civilizations. The surplus food produced by agricultural communities allowed for population growth and urbanization, facilitating the development of trade, arts, and sciences. The ability to sustain large populations and support specialized labor enabled the construction of monumental structures, the creation of written languages, and the establishment of centralized governments. These advancements laid the foundation for the rise of powerful empires and the flourishing of human cultures.

In conclusion the start of agriculture was a defining moment in human history, transforming the way people lived, worked, and interacted with their environment. The transition from hunting and gathering to farming allowed for the development of settled communities, the accumulation of surplus food, and the specialization of labor. These changes laid the foundation for the rise of complex societies and the development of civilization. The legacy of early agriculture is still evident today, as the practices and innovations of ancient farmers continue to shape our world. From the food we eat to the cities we live in, the impact of agriculture is all-encompassing, highlighting the ingenuity and adaptability of our species. Agriculture remains a cornerstone of human civilization, supporting the growth of modern societies and enabling the advancements that define contemporary life. The innovations and practices developed by early farmers continue to influence agricultural techniques and food production methods today, underscoring the enduring significance of the agricultural revolution in shaping human history.

CHAPTER 9:

SOCIAL STRUCTURES AND GOVERNANCE

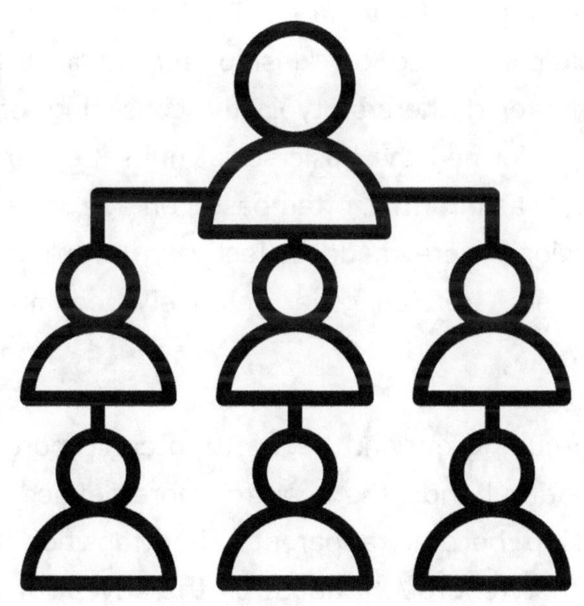

Introduction: The Birth of Social Structures:

The evolution of social structures and governance systems was a critical milestone in human history, shaping the way communities organized, interacted, and governed themselves. As Homo sapiens transitioned from nomadic hunter-gatherer groups to settled agricultural societies, the complexity of their social interactions increased, necessitating more structured forms of organization and leadership. This chapter explores the origins and evolution of social hierarchies, leadership roles, and governance systems, highlighting their impact on the stability and complexity of early human societies.

Early Social Organization:

In the early stages of human society, social organization was relatively simple, based on kinship and familial ties. Small bands of hunter-gatherers, typically consisting of extended family groups, formed the basic social units. Leadership within these groups was informal, often based on age, experience, and ability. Decisions were made collectively, with input from all adult members, reflecting a relatively egalitarian social structure.

As these groups grew and began to interact more frequently with neighboring bands, the need for more defined social roles and leadership became apparent. The transition to a more sedentary lifestyle, brought about by the advent of agriculture, further accelerated this process. Permanent settlements required systems to manage resources, coordinate communal activities, and resolve conflicts. These changes laid the groundwork for more complex social hierarchies and governance systems.

The Rise of Social Hierarchies:

The establishment of agricultural communities led to the accumulation of surplus food and resources, which in turn allowed for population growth and the development of social hierarchies. These hierarchies were often based on control over land, resources, and labor. Individuals or groups who could manage these assets effectively gained power and authority. In many early societies, social hierarchies were reinforced by religious or spiritual beliefs. Leaders were often seen as divinely chosen or possessing special connections to the spiritual world, which helped legitimize their authority and maintain social order.

The construction of monumental architecture, such as temples and pyramids, served both religious and political purposes, demonstrating the leader's power and the society's collective strength. These structures not only showcased the leader's ability to mobilize resources and labor but also acted as centers of religious and social activities, further solidifying their role in the community.

Development of Governance Systems:

As societies continued to grow, the need for more formal governance systems became apparent. Early forms of government were often based on tribal or clan structures, with councils of elders or chiefs making decisions for the community.

These councils provided a means of organizing communal activities, managing resources, and resolving disputes. Over time, these systems evolved into more centralized forms of governance, with kings, pharaohs, or emperors wielding significant power.

 The development of writing systems was a crucial factor in the evolution of governance. Written records allowed for the codification of laws, administrative procedures, and historical events. This increased the efficiency and consistency of governance, enabling the management of larger and more complex societies. Early legal codes, such as the Code of Hammurabi, exemplify how written laws helped standardize justice and maintain order within growing communities.

Codification of Laws and Written Records:

 The codification of laws and the maintenance of written records were pivotal in the establishment of governance systems. Early societies recognized the importance of creating standardized rules to govern behavior, resolve conflicts, and protect property rights. The introduction of written legal codes provided a clear and consistent framework for justice, reducing the potential for arbitrary or biased decision-making.

 Written records also played a vital role in administration and governance. They enabled the efficient collection of taxes, management of resources, and organization of large-scale projects, such as irrigation systems and public works. The ability to record and transmit information across generations ensured the continuity and stability of governance structures, contributing to the longevity and resilience of early civilizations.

Formation of Early States and Empires:

 The development of social structures and governance systems paved the way for the formation of early states and empires. As agricultural societies expanded, they often absorbed or conquered neighboring communities, creating larger political entities. The consolidation of power under centralized leadership allowed for the coordination of extensive territories and diverse populations.

 Early states and empires employed various strategies to maintain control and integrate their subjects. These included the establishment of administrative hierarchies, the construction of infrastructure to facilitate communication and trade, and the promotion of a unified cultural or religious identity. The rise of powerful empires, such as those in Mesopotamia, Egypt, and the Indus Valley, exemplifies how effective governance and social organization contributed to the development of complex and influential civilizations.

Impact on Daily Life and Society:

 The evolution of social structures and governance had profound impacts on the daily lives of individuals and the overall functioning of society. With the establishment of hierarchical systems, people's roles and statuses became more defined, influencing their access to resources, opportunities, and social mobility. The emergence of specialized professions allowed individuals to pursue various occupations, contributing to the diversification of skills and knowledge within the community.

Governance systems also played a critical role in maintaining social order and stability. The enforcement of laws and regulations helped protect individuals' rights and property, fostering a sense of security and predictability. Public projects, such as infrastructure development and the provision of social services, improved the quality of life and supported the growth and prosperity of communities.

Legacy of Early Social Structures and Governance:

The evolution of social structures and governance systems was a defining moment in human history, transforming the way people organized themselves, managed resources, and interacted with one another. These developments laid the foundation for the rise of complex societies and civilizations, enabling the growth of population centers, the specialization of labor, and the creation of sophisticated cultural, economic, and political institutions. The legacy of these early systems is still evident today, as the principles of social organization and governance continue to shape modern societies and influence the way we live and govern ourselves.

CHAPTER 10:

THE GREAT BOTTLENECK

Before ending the book by entering the known history, we need to take a step back approximately 70,000 years ago to discuss a critical event in human evolution. This event brought Homo sapiens perilously close to extinction and serves as a stark reminder of our species' vulnerability and resilience. This chapter, aptly named "The Great Bottleneck," aims to parallel the "How They Became Extinct" chapters from the previous books, highlighting that even Homo sapiens faced near extinction. This chapter is not about the Cold War, where the threat of nuclear annihilation loomed, but rather an ancient, natural catastrophe that almost wiped out our ancestors.

The Toba Catastrophe Theory:

Around 74,000 years ago, the supervolcanic eruption of Mount Toba in present-day Indonesia is believed to have caused a massive environmental crisis. The Toba eruption is one of the largest known volcanic events on Earth, ejecting an estimated 2,800 cubic kilometers of volcanic material. This event had a profound impact on global climate, leading to what is known as a "volcanic winter." The ash and sulfur dioxide released into the atmosphere by the Toba eruption significantly reduced sunlight reaching the Earth's surface, resulting in a dramatic drop in temperatures. This prolonged period of cooling, possibly lasting several years, severely affected the global climate, disrupting ecosystems and food sources. For Homo sapiens, who were primarily hunter-gatherers relying on the availability of plants and animals, this environmental upheaval presented a dire challenge. The consequences of such a volcanic winter would have been devastating, causing drastic shifts in weather patterns, reduced plant growth, and significant losses in animal populations, thereby making survival increasingly difficult for early human communities.

Population Bottleneck:

The environmental stress caused by the Toba eruption is thought to have led to a significant reduction in the human population. Genetic studies suggest that the human population might have dwindled to as few as 1,000 to 10,000 breeding individuals, creating a population bottleneck. This was dangerously low, roughly equivalent to less than half the capacity of a typical NBA basketball stadium. Such a drastic reduction in numbers had profound implications for the genetic diversity of our species. A population bottleneck can increase the effects of genetic drift, reduce genetic variation, and increase the likelihood of inbreeding, which can further compromise a population's ability to adapt to environmental changes. The reduced genetic diversity among modern humans is often attributed to this bottleneck event, which serves as a pivotal point in our evolutionary history. The impact of this bottleneck is still evident today, as the relatively low genetic variation among modern human populations suggests a period of severe constriction in our ancestral gene pool.

The significance of this population bottleneck cannot be overstated. It represents a period when the survival of our species hung in the balance, and only through a combination of adaptability, resourcefulness, and perhaps a bit of luck did Homo sapiens manage to endure. The genetic bottleneck also means that modern humans are more genetically similar to each other than many other species, which has implications for our understanding of human evolution and the spread of genetic traits. Just thinking about it, it was really close—just a virus, a small asteroid, or any other catastrophic event could have driven Homo sapiens to extinction.

Surviving the Bottleneck:

Despite the severity of the Toba eruption and the ensuing volcanic winter, Homo sapiens managed to survive. The resilience of our species during this period is a testament to our adaptability and resourcefulness. Survival strategies likely included migration to more hospitable areas, diversification of food sources, and the development of social structures that facilitated cooperation and resource sharing. The Toba catastrophe likely forced human populations to innovate and adapt to the harsh conditions. These adaptations may have included the development of new tools, clothing, and shelter to cope with the colder climate. Additionally, the need for cooperation and communal support would have reinforced social bonds and the importance of group cohesion, laying the groundwork for more complex social structures in the future. It is likely that during this time, early humans developed sophisticated hunting strategies, improved their tool-making techniques, and formed stronger social bonds that enabled them to share resources more effectively.

The survival of Homo sapiens through this period can also be attributed to their ability to exploit a variety of environments and resources. While some groups may have migrated to warmer, more fertile regions, others developed new ways to utilize the resources available in their existing habitats. This period of adversity likely accelerated technological and social innovations, driving the development of more efficient hunting tools, improved shelter construction, and more effective means of clothing and protecting themselves against the harsh climate.

Implications for Modern Humans:

The Great Bottleneck had lasting effects on the genetic makeup of modern humans. The reduced genetic diversity resulting from this event means that all modern humans are more closely related than we might otherwise be if such a bottleneck had not occurred. This genetic similarity can be seen in the relatively low genetic variation between human populations compared to other species, think of it like this: the closer related you are to your partner, the higher the risk for passing down a genetic disease to the baby. The smaller the population, the closer we were to extinction. Furthermore, understanding the Great Bottleneck provides insights into the resilience and adaptability of Homo sapiens. It highlights our ability to survive and thrive despite facing extreme challenges. This period in our history underscores the importance of adaptability, innovation, and social cohesion—traits that continue to define our species today. The lessons learned from this bottleneck event emphasize the critical role of adaptability and innovation in human survival, and how these traits have enabled our species to navigate and overcome some of the most challenging periods in our evolutionary history.

In addition to these genetic implications, the Great Bottleneck also had a profound impact on the cultural and social development of Homo sapiens. The challenges faced during this period likely fostered a greater sense of community and cooperation, as small, isolated groups had to rely heavily on each other for survival. This increased social cohesion may have laid the foundation for the complex social structures that would later emerge as human societies continued to grow and develop.

Conclusion: The Dawn of a Resilient Species:

The Great Bottleneck serves as a crucial chapter in the story of Homo sapiens, illustrating the vulnerability and resilience of our species. By surviving this near-extinction event, our ancestors demonstrated the adaptability and ingenuity that have become hallmarks of human evolution. As we prepare to move forward and explore the dawn of writing and recorded history, it is essential to recognize that our journey was fraught with challenges that shaped our development and prepared us for the complex societies we would eventually build. This chapter not only parallels the extinction narratives of other Homo species but also sets the stage for the emergence of sophisticated civilizations. The ability to overcome such a significant population crisis speaks volumes about the inherent strength and potential of Homo sapiens, paving the way for the remarkable achievements that would follow in recorded history. Our survival through the Great Bottleneck is a testament to the extraordinary resilience and adaptive capacity of our species, traits that have continued to drive human progress and innovation throughout history. As we conclude our exploration of prehistory, it is important to reflect on how these early challenges and triumphs have shaped the path of human evolution, setting the stage for the dawn of recorded history.

The story of the Great Bottleneck is not just one of survival, but of thriving against all odds. It serves as a reminder that even in the face of seemingly insurmountable challenges, the human spirit, characterized by resilience, creativity, and cooperation, can prevail. This chapter exemplifies how the crucible of adversity has forged a species capable of remarkable achievements, setting the foundation for the rich tapestry of human history that would unfold in the millennia to come. As we stand on the cusp of the known history, reflecting on this pivotal event helps us appreciate the incredible journey our ancestors undertook to ensure the continuity and prosperity of Homo sapiens.

CHAPTER II:

THE DAWN OF WRITING AND RECORDED HISTORY

Writing represents the transition from prehistory to recorded history, enabling humans to document events, communicate complex ideas, and preserve knowledge across generations. While agriculture is the biggest transformation event in humankind, writing is the transformation from prehistory to known history, from ancient humans to modern humans.

Writing began as a system of pictographs and ideographs used to represent objects, concepts, and sounds. The earliest known writing system is cuneiform, developed by the Sumerians in Mesopotamia around 3400 BCE. Cuneiform started as simple pictographs inscribed on clay tablets and evolved into a sophisticated script used for various administrative, economic, and literary purposes. The Sumerians used cuneiform to keep records of transactions, codify laws, and compose epic literature like the "Epic of Gilgamesh." This script facilitated the administration of their cities and the coordination of large-scale agricultural projects, contributing to the rise of one of the world's first great civilizations.

Simultaneously, in ancient Egypt, hieroglyphics emerged around 3100 BCE. This writing system combined logographic and alphabetic elements, allowing for the representation of both concrete and abstract concepts. Hieroglyphics were extensively used in religious texts, monumental inscriptions, and administrative records. The Egyptians believed that writing was a gift from the god Thoth and used it to record their spiritual and cultural heritage. Hieroglyphics were not only engraved on temple walls and obelisks but also meticulously inscribed on papyrus scrolls and coffins, ensuring that every aspect of Egyptian life, from mundane daily activities to grand religious rituals, was documented. The construction of pyramids and the intricate carvings on tombs are testaments to the importance of writing in preserving the legacy of the pharaohs and their divine right to rule. These monumental structures, adorned with hieroglyphic inscriptions, served both as eternal resting places for the pharaohs and as lasting records of their achievements and divine status. Hieroglyphics played a crucial role in maintaining the continuity of Egyptian culture and administration over millennia, reflecting a civilization deeply invested in the power of the written word to convey authority, preserve history, and communicate with the gods.

In the Indus Valley, another early writing system appeared around 2500 BCE. Although the script remains undeciphered, it is clear that it was used for administrative and possibly ritualistic purposes, reflecting the complexity and organization of the society. The Harappan script, found on seals, pottery, and other artifacts, indicates a highly developed urban culture with trade connections extending to Mesopotamia and beyond. The inscriptions on these seals often depict a variety of symbols and motifs, suggesting a rich and complex symbolic language. The widespread use of this script across numerous sites within the Indus Valley Civilization implies a centralized administration capable of managing resources and coordinating large urban centers. These cities, known for their advanced urban planning, included features such as sophisticated drainage systems, granaries, and standardized weights and measures. The presence of the Harappan script on objects related to trade and administration highlights the role of writing in facilitating economic transactions and maintaining social order.

Additionally, the script's use in possible ritual contexts suggests it may have played a part in the spiritual and cultural practices of the Harappan people, further emphasizing its significance in this ancient civilization.

The Spread of Writing:

As writing systems developed, they spread across regions through trade, conquest, and cultural exchange. The Phoenicians, known for their maritime trading networks, played a crucial role in disseminating writing. They developed an alphabetic script around 1200 BCE, which greatly influenced the Greek and Latin alphabets, forming the basis for many modern writing systems. The simplicity and efficiency of the Phoenician alphabet made it accessible and adaptable, facilitating widespread literacy and record-keeping. The Greeks adopted and modified the Phoenician script, adding vowels, which enhanced its utility and adaptability to various languages.

In China, writing began with oracle bone script during the Shang Dynasty around 1200 BCE. This early script was primarily used for divination, inscribed on animal bones and turtle shells, and provided valuable insights into the political, social, and religious life of the Shang Dynasty. Over time, this script evolved into Chinese characters, which remain in use today. The spread of writing in China played a crucial role in facilitating the administration of a vast empire and preserving its rich cultural heritage. Chinese characters were utilized to record historical events, philosophical teachings, and scientific advancements, thus contributing to the continuity and cohesion of Chinese civilization. The development of paper during the

Han Dynasty further revolutionized the spread and preservation of written knowledge, offering a more accessible and durable medium compared to earlier materials like silk and bamboo strips. This innovation led to the proliferation of books, government documents, and private correspondences, significantly increasing literacy and the dissemination of knowledge. The invention of paper not only aided in the preservation of Chinese cultural and intellectual achievements but also enhanced the administrative efficiency of the empire, enabling more effective governance and communication across vast distances.

The spread of writing also reached the Americas, where the Maya developed a complex hieroglyphic script around 300 BCE. This sophisticated writing system consisted of over 800 individual glyphs, each representing different sounds, words, or concepts. The Maya used writing extensively to document their history, astronomy, and religious practices, inscribing texts on a variety of materials including stone monuments, pottery, and bark-paper codices. Their intricate inscriptions on stelae, temple walls, and codices provide valuable insights into their sophisticated knowledge and cultural achievements. These records reveal detailed accounts of dynastic histories, political events, and mythological narratives, showcasing the depth and richness of Maya civilization. The use of writing in astronomical calculations and calendrical systems demonstrates the Maya's advanced understanding of celestial phenomena and timekeeping. They developed complex calendars, such as the Haab' and Tzolk'in, and accurately predicted solar and lunar eclipses, solstices, and equinoxes. The Maya's ability to integrate their knowledge of astronomy with their religious and agricultural practices underscores the significance of writing in preserving and disseminating critical information across generations.

Impact on Society:

The advent of writing had profound impacts on early societies. It enabled the creation of legal codes, such as the Code of Hammurabi in Babylon, which established a framework for justice and governance. Writing also facilitated the administration of complex economies, allowing for the recording of transactions, inventories, and tax records. The ability to keep detailed records ensured the efficient management of resources and the stability of the state. Written contracts and legal documents provided a basis for the regulation of trade and property, fostering economic growth and social stability.

In addition to its practical applications, writing enriched cultural and intellectual life. It allowed for the recording of religious texts, literature, and scientific knowledge. Epic tales like the "Epic of Gilgamesh," religious scriptures like the "Rigveda," and philosophical works like those of Confucius and Laozi have been preserved through writing, offering insights into the beliefs, values, and knowledge of ancient civilizations. The preservation of these texts has allowed subsequent generations to learn from and build upon the intellectual achievements of their predecessors. Written literature, poetry, and historical records became essential in shaping cultural identities and preserving the collective memory of societies.

Writing and the Development of Civilization:

The development of writing systems was integral to the rise of civilizations. It enabled the centralization of power, the administration of large territories, and the coordination of complex social structures. Writing facilitated communication across distances, the preservation of history, and the transmission of culture and knowledge. The ability to record and transmit information contributed to the development of education and the professionalization of scribes, scholars, and administrators. Educational institutions and libraries became centers of learning and knowledge preservation, playing a crucial role in the intellectual and cultural development of societies.

Written records allowed for the accumulation and advancement of knowledge, fostering scientific and technological progress. The recording of astronomical observations, mathematical calculations, and medical treatments enabled early scientists and scholars to develop sophisticated understandings of the natural world. The spread of written knowledge through trade and cultural exchange further accelerated technological innovation and cultural development. Innovations in writing materials, such as papyrus, parchment, and paper, facilitated the dissemination and preservation of written works.

Writing also played a critical role in the development of legal and administrative systems. Written laws provided a consistent and transparent framework for governance, ensuring fairness and accountability. Administrative records enabled the efficient management of resources and the coordination of large-scale public works, such as irrigation systems and infrastructure projects. These advancements contributed to the stability and prosperity of early civilizations, laying the groundwork for the complex societies that would follow. The ability to maintain detailed records of economic transactions and population data supported the growth of trade and commerce, enhancing the interconnectedness and complexity of early economies.

Conclusion: The Threshold of History:

The dawn of writing and recorded history marks the end of prehistory and the beginning of a new era. Through writing, humans gained the ability to document their experiences, share their knowledge, and build upon the achievements of previous generations. This transformative development laid the foundation for the complex, interconnected world we live in today. The resilience, adaptability, and ingenuity of Homo sapiens enabled us to overcome countless challenges and achieve remarkable progress.

"And after that, the known history started and everything we know."

Conclusion

This book has explored the remarkable transformation of Homo sapiens from their earliest days to the dawn of recorded history. Our ancestors demonstrated extraordinary adaptability and ingenuity, from developing rudimentary tools and mastering fire to establishing early social structures. These advancements laid the foundation for complex societies and the eventual rise of civilizations.

For tens of thousands of years, Homo sapiens lived exclusively in Africa, hunting, running, hiding, and surviving. We emerged from Africa and gradually spread across the world, adapting to various environments and overcoming countless challenges. The Great Bottleneck event drastically reduced our population to possibly as few as a thousand individuals, but from this small group, we have grown to a global population of 8 billion today.

The advent of agriculture marked a pivotal shift, transforming human societies from nomadic hunter-gatherers to settled agriculturalists. This transition facilitated population growth, permanent settlements, and intricate social hierarchies. The development of trade networks, specialized labor, and agricultural innovations allowed early communities to thrive and evolve into sophisticated urban centers. This period saw the rise of distinct social classes and the creation of governance structures that supported large populations.

However, it was the invention of writing that truly revolutionized human civilization. Writing enabled meticulous documentation, communication of complex ideas, and preservation of knowledge across generations. Early writing systems played crucial roles in administration, cultural expression, and scientific advancement. Writing facilitated the codification of laws, recording of astronomical observations, medical knowledge, and technological innovations, ensuring that valuable information was not lost but accumulated over time.

Reflecting on our journey through prehistory, it is evident that the resilience, adaptability, and creativity of our ancestors have profoundly shaped human history. The transition from prehistory to the dawn of writing and recorded history marks the culmination of countless challenges and triumphs that defined our early development. As we stand on the threshold of recorded history, we recognize that the legacy of our prehistoric ancestors continues to influence and inspire us. Their remarkable journey laid the foundation for the rich and diverse tapestry of human civilization that continues to evolve. The dawn of writing signifies not just the end of prehistory but the beginning of an era where human knowledge and culture could be meticulously preserved and widely shared, establishing the interconnected and complex world we inhabit today.

This is the story of Homo sapiens, the story of 117 billion people across history, the story of everything. From a vulnerable species to the dominant inhabitants of Earth

Thank You

This is the end of the "Origins: The Evolution of Homo Species" series. I hope this series of six books has given you an idea of who we are and where we came from. I hope the beginnings with Homo habilis taught you about our humble origins. I hope Homo erectus, with their migration, control of fire, and long lifespan, showed you how quickly we can advance. I hope Homo heidelbergensis, with their hunting techniques, demonstrated that even with smaller bodies, we can take down beasts. I hope the Denisovans and Neanderthals, with their interbreeding and intelligence, taught you that we are not very different from them. I hope our past and the story of Emma and Rayan illustrated how wonderful and hard the journey was. Most importantly, I hope all these books taught you that we were not alone on this journey; this is not just the story of other Homo species but the story of us, of me and you.

Thank you for completing this journey with me. Although it was a long one, I learned and enjoyed it immensely. Thank you, and I will see you in another work.

Glossary of Terms

Atlatl:
- A spear-thrower that provides leverage to hurl spears with greater force and precision.

Aurignacian Culture:
- An archaeological culture of the Upper Paleolithic, associated with early modern humans in Europe, known for advanced tools and symbolic artifacts.

Bering Land Bridge (Beringia):
- A land bridge that connected Asia and North America during periods of lower sea levels, allowing human migration.

Blade Technology:
- The creation of long, thin stone blades used for a variety of tools, indicative of advanced craftsmanship and understanding of materials.

Cave Paintings:
- Early forms of artistic expression found in caves, depicting animals, human figures, and abstract symbols, often associated with spiritual or ritual significance.

Clovis Points:
- Distinctive, fluted projectile points used by early inhabitants of the Americas, indicative of advanced hunting technologies.

Cuneiform:
- One of the earliest known writing systems, developed by the Sumerians in Mesopotamia around 3400 BCE, used for administrative, economic, and literary purposes.

Domestication:
- The process by which humans cultivate plants and breed animals for specific traits, leading to genetic changes in the species.

Epic of Gilgamesh:
- An ancient Mesopotamian epic poem, one of the earliest known works of literary writing.

Fertile Crescent:
- A region in the Middle East where some of the earliest known agricultural communities and civilizations emerged.

Levallois Technique:
- A distinctive method of stone tool production used by early humans, involving the preparation of a core to produce uniformly shaped flakes.

Ochre:
- A natural clay earth pigment used by early humans for decoration, artistic expression, and possibly symbolic purposes.

Pictographs:
- Simple drawings or paintings on rock surfaces representing objects, concepts, or sounds, an early form of writing.

Venus Figurines:
- Prehistoric statuettes of women, often with exaggerated physical features, believed to represent fertility or mother goddesses.

References

"Sapiens: A Brief History of Humankind" by Yuval Noah Harari, Harper

"The Cambridge Encyclopedia of Human Evolution" edited by Steve Jones, Robert Martin, and David Pilbeam, Cambridge University Press

"Who We Are and How We Got Here: Ancient DNA and the New Science of the Human Past" by David Reich, Pantheon

"The Greatest Show on Earth: The Evidence for Evolution" by Richard Dawkins, Free Press

"The First Human: The Race to Discover Our Earliest Ancestors" by Ann Gibbons, Anchor

www.ingramcontent.com/pod-product-compliance
Lightning Source LLC
Chambersburg PA
CBHW071045250726
48653CB00005B/2016